The Professional Astrologer's NCGR-PAA

Education Curriculum
And
Study Guide
for
Certification Testing

Originally written and compiled by the 2003 NCGR Board of Examiners under the direction of Bruce Scofield

Revised and edited in 2008 and 2015
by Shirley Soffer, NCGR-PAA Education Director
and Bruce Scofield, President

National Council for Geocosmic Research, Inc.
Professional Astrologers' Alliance

© 2015 National Council for Geocosmic Research, Inc. and
NCGR Professional Astrologers' Alliance, Inc.
All rights reserved

No part of this book may be reproduced or transmitted in any form or by any means, electronic or mechanical, including photocopying, scanning, recording or by any information storage and retrieval system, without written permission from the publisher. Direct requests and inquiries to: education@astrologersalliance.org

ISBN: 978-0-61529-639-5
Current Edition Printed 2015
Production and layout: Loretta Lopez
Illustrations: Bruce Scofield
Revised / Updated Cover Design by Loretta Lopez
(Based on original cover design by A.T. Mann & Mark Kunzel)

Published by The National Council for Geocosmic Research and NCGR Professional Astrologers' Alliance, Inc.
www.geocosmic.org
www.astrologersalliance.org

Printed in the United States of America

The original NCGR Curriculum resulted from a national education conference held at Princeton University in August 1979. Teachers from throughout the United States representing the major astrological disciplines devised a four-year study program encompassing modern and traditional concepts.

With the formation of the NCGR-Professional Astrologers' Alliance (PAA) in 2008, this same NCGR Curriculum is transferred to the NCGR-PAA in its entirety

Contents

- 7   Foreword
- 9   NCGR-PAA Curriculum
- 13   Study Guide for Level I
- 47   Study Guide for Level II
- 78   Study Guide for Level III
- 104   Study Guide for Level IV
- 122   Appendix I:
  The NCGR-PAA Code of Ethics
- 131   Applendix II
  Calculating a Horoscope
- 149   Appendix III
  The History of Astrology
- 165   Program for Applying Schools Equivalency Criteria
- 170   The Formation of the NCGR Professional Astrologers' Alliance

Foreword

A Brief History of NCGR's Original Education Program

NCGR's Education and Certification Program, recognized internationally for its rigor and excellence since 1979, is one of NCGR's major achievements. This evolving program continued under the aegis of NCGR until it became apparent that certain aspects of it were in conflict with federal tax codes. In 2008 the NCGR-Professional Astrologers' Alliance (PAA) was formed and NCGR's prior certification program was transferred to the new organization in its entirety, thus continuing NCGR's historic educational program begun more than a quarter of a century ago. The NCGR-PAA today administers the four Levels of certification testing based on the same educational curriculum as before and as now found in this newly designed Study Guide.

The origins of the NCGR-PAA Education and Certification Program are located in the 1970's. After several years of preliminary planning within the NCGR Board, led by successive Directors of Education Ken Negus, Lenore Canter, Joan Negus, and Joanna Shannon, a national education conference was held at the Princeton University campus in August, 1979. About 50 professional astrologers and teachers of astrology from throughout the United States, including delegates from NCGR's local chapters, gathered for a five-day meeting to create and launch an educational program. After the framework of the curriculum was established through a democratic process at the conference, a National Education Committee of ten members was entrusted with the task of creating four Levels of tests, writing a Study Guide, and giving examinations. Over the years, the Education Committee continued the work of updating and revising the curriculum and tests, including a total revision of the Study Guide in 2003 along with revised tests on all four Levels.

NCGR's program was structured in four successive Levels because it was envisioned that someday astrology might be once again studied in colleges and universities and much discussion was focused on which astrological methodologies might be studied during each of the four years of a typical college education. From the outset it was envisioned that within a major in astrology, the student would also take courses that would support his or her intended specialty, such as psychology for consulting astrologers, economics, history, business and finance for mundane astrologers, and statistics for research astrologers.

Though the focus was on technique, the Education Committee members were well aware that most astrologers do some consulting regardless of whether they have had any formal training in that area or not, and it would take many years to realize their vision of astrology within collegiate programs with appropriate supplementary course work. Because of that, it was decided to recommend that astrologers acquire counseling skills and to include questions that required knowledge of and sensitivity to ethics in counseling in each of the four levels of testing questions.

NCGR's original Education and Certification Program has withstood the test of time. It has been implemented throughout the United States, in Mexico, Turkey, Thailand, and in several other countries. With its outgrowth into the newly-formed NCGR-PAA, the program continues forward, anticipating future growth and development. With pride and pleasure NCGR-PAA presents this newly-designed, revised, and edited 2015 edition of the Education Curriculum and Study Guide for Certification Testing.

Bruce Scofield, C.A., NCGR-PAA
President

NCGR-PAA Curriculum

The NCGR-PAA education program is designed to give structure to astrological studies in order to raise the standards of the field for both students and teachers. It is designed to be used as a framework for an astrology major in a four-year college curriculum. While NCGR and NCGR-PAA offer workshops, lectures, webinars, and other programs, additional educational opportunities are available through approved schools (see appendix), regional and national astrology conferences, master classes, and selected NCGR chapter programs.

The NCGR-PAA curriculum is built on a 20th Century synthesis of astrological concepts and methodologies which at the time of its creation were, for the most part, the norm for practitioners in the United States. This synthesis is founded on the writings and teachings of a number of well-known astrologers from England and the United States, a long list that includes Alan Leo, Charles Carter, Dane Rudhyar, Marc Edmond Jones, and many others. In addition, attention is given to the remarkable innovations (midpoints, planetary pictures, dials, composite charts, etc.) of the German astrologers, including Witte and Ebertin. Since the original conception of the curriculum, Classical Astrology, a general term encompassing the astrology practiced in Greek, Roman, Medieval and Renaissance times has become popular and some Classical concepts have been incorporated into the study guide and exams. In addition, the curriculum recognizes the need for certified astrologers to know something about Hindu/Vedic astrology, and the Chinese and Mesoamerican astrological traditions. In this way, the NCGR-PAA education program strives to keep abreast of trends in the larger astrological community and also to draw attention to astrology as a tradition that has roots in cultures other than that of the West.

Astrology is presented in the NCGR-PAA curriculum as a subject that not only includes its practice, but also its scientific and technical foundations, and its history. The existence of a research component in Level IV was designed to encourage critical thinking and interest in astrology as a testable subject and to advance geocosmic research. The astronomy of the solar system and the use of astronomical coordinate systems are studied on each level, becoming increasingly more detailed as the student progresses. The curriculum strives to keep its content free of any association with religions or metaphysical assumptions.

The majority of the subject matter of the NCGR-PAA curriculum is concerned with the astronomical basis and psychological or practical interpretation of the horoscope. The horoscope (view of the hour) is the traditional term for a chart calculated for a specific time and place. It is literally a map of the sky at one precise moment and location. Today, the horoscope of a person is often referred to as a "birth chart" while the horoscope for an occurrence is referred to as an "event chart." The mathematics for the construction of the horoscope is consistent with the methods used in astronomy, navigation, and surveying. The components of the horoscope, the planets, signs, houses, and aspects, are the traditional subject matter of practical astrology and consulting astrologers use this information in their work.

This study guide is your key to preparation for the exams. All the material on the exams, at each level, is found in this document. Prospective exam takers should deepen their understanding of the various topics through readings (see bibliography) or through classes, many of which are specifically tailored to the curriculum

Level I

Level I focuses on the building blocks in the foundation of Western astrology. In order to pass a proficiency examination at this level the student must be familiar with the signs, planets, houses, intersection points (Ascendant, MC, Moon's Nodes), major aspects and their configurations; and be able to apply them in a simple natal interpretation. Some knowledge of the basics of Classical Astrology is also required at this level. In addition the student must know how to calculate a natal chart by hand (no computer) for any geographical location. The astronomy topics introduced on Level I include the solar system, eclipses, retrograde motion, and solstices.

Level II

On **Level II**, natal delineation is further developed and minor aspects, lunar phases, derived houses, asteroids, and fixed stars are added to broaden interpretation. The dynamic elements of astrology (which include transits, progressions, and solar arcs) are also introduced at this level. Additional elements of Classical Astrology are covered. Various systems of house division are compared. Calculations include relocation charts, transits, progressions, solar arc directions, declinations, the Vertex, the Equatorial Ascendant, and antiscia (symmetry around the solstice points). Some acquaintance with mundane charting such as ingress charts is required at this level, but is covered more fully in Level III.

Level III

Level III covers the subjects of horary and electional astrology, synastry, composite charts, solar and lunar returns and introduces the concepts and usage of the 360° and 90° dials associated with the German schools (Hamburg/Uranian and Cosmobiology). The history of astrology is also covered in detail at this level and some familiarity with other astrological traditions, specifically Vedic, Chinese and, Mesoamerican, is expected. A take-home test on electional and mundane astrology is required.

Level IV

Level IV solidifies the information of the other levels and adds rectification (which can incorporate many techniques). Once rectification is passed, the student may specialize in consulting, instruction, scientific research, or general research.

Fees vary with the level of testing, and with the stages and tracks of Levels III and IV. For full information, please go to the Certification section of the NCGR-PAA website:

www.astrologersalliance.org

or e-mail: education@astrologersalliance.org

Study Guide for Level I

The basic symbolism of astrology: planets, signs, houses and aspects. Special conditions, both modern and traditional, that modify planetary action. Ethics. Horoscope calculation. Astronomical foundations of astrology.

Introduction to Astrology

Astrology is a subject that studies, and applies in practice, connections between the astronomical environment and Earth's dynamic processes including individual life, collective life, weather, climate, tides, geological changes, etc. It is not limited to the analysis of human personality and life history. In contrast, dictionaries often define astrology only as a study that attempts to understand the affairs of human beings by studying the stars and planets. In essence, the most popular branch of astrology, natal astrology, is exactly that. Astrologers are able to read character and destiny from a map of the sky computed for the time and place of birth, a map called the horoscope. The positions of the planets in the horoscope have long been known to symbolize a person's basic character, prominent personality traits, and also provide the timing of major life events. Over the centuries astrological techniques have evolved and, in addition to the above, a good astrologer is also able to deduce something about a person's spouse, parents, children, and even pets from that person's horoscope.

Ptolemy (c. 150 AD), one of the greatest scientists of the ancient world and author of the major astrological work, *Tetrabiblos*, divided astrology into two fundamental categories: universal and genethlialogical. The former was concerned with natural phenomena such as climate, weather, earthquakes, agriculture, plagues, etc. The latter was concerned with the affairs of individuals. By the Renaissance these two branches were known as natural and judicial astrology, respectively. Many of the founders of modern science either practiced natural astrology or had no quarrel with it. In modern times this branch has also been called mundane astrology and its area of inquiry was extended to history, politics, and the fates of nations. Judicial astrology was and is far more controversial. Traditionally, this branch included natal astrology, horary astrology, and electional astrology, all of which deal with the life patterns and experiences of humans. In modern times, the astrology of individuals is called natal astrology, and horary and electional are sometimes called judicial astrology.

An understanding of astrology begins with the concept that it is basically a system, code, or language that uses symbols in four basic categories: the Sun, Moon and planets, zodiac signs, houses, and aspects. These symbols correspond to very specific categories of things, events, arenas of life, as well as personality traits. An astrologer blends combinations of these symbols and makes deductions about a person or situation. This act of interpretation is gleaned from a long tradition of knowledge and experience. Familiarity with astronomy is also necessary in order to create the schematic map of the sky commonly called the horoscope. Astrologers use astronomical data, mathematics, and computers to determine precisely how the sky was or will be configured at a given place and time.

Astrology as a subject differs from hard sciences like physics or chemistry in several ways. First, its body of knowledge used in practice is mostly empirical, that is, as it was developed over time by generations of practitioners. Second, astrology receives no institutional support or funding and this results in minimal scientific research. In regard to other modern scientifically-informed subjects, astrology can best be compared to medicine or psychology, both of which use technical knowledge along with personal judgment calls. Astrology as a practice, like medicine and psychology, is a diagnostic art that makes use of technical data that is then applied to the human condition. Where astrology differs radically from conventional Western science is its use of a holistic kind of logic, one that assumes that things are interconnected. Conventional Western science is concerned with physical separations and boundaries that can be measured exactly. Astrology is concerned with complex systems (e.g, the body and mind) and how the emergent properties of these systems respond to the dynamics of the cosmic environment. Astrology works with correlations and linkages and as a practice is concerned with the ecology of body, mind, and spirit on this planet. Astrology is not anti-science, however, and newer emerging branches of systems science may turn out to be receptive to astrology.

Modern astrology, based on more than 4,000 years of observations that have been constantly revised and updated, has generally retained its continuity with an earlier time when humankind was not separate from nature. Just as ancient medicine is not the medicine practiced today, ancient Mesopotamian or Medieval astrology is not the astrology of contemporary times. Astrology has evolved over time, meeting the needs of each historical era, and in the process both gaining and losing methodologies. Astrology continues to prove its value today as it has done for millenia. In modern times, much has been added to the evolving astrological paradigm from other subjects such as psychology, medicine, economics and ecology.

Core Astrological Symbolism:

Planets

Planets represent or symbolize archetypal functions, motivating energies, and fundamental principles of nature and life. Note: the Sun and Moon are not planets (the Sun is a star and the Moon is a satellite) though it has become a tradition in astrology to group them with the planets and refer to all of them as such. Although Pluto has recently been reclassified by the International Astronomical Union as a dwarf planet, we are including it here as it has long been standard practice in astrology to include it in horoscopic analysis.

Glyphs

☉ — Sun
☽ — Moon
☿ — Mercury
♀ — Venus
♂ — Mars
♃ — Jupiter
♄ — Saturn
♅ — Uranus
♆ — Neptune
♇ — Pluto

Descriptive Keywords

Sun — vitality, ego, the individual will, sense of purpose, well-being, personal power, creativity, pride, self-image, leadership, authority, males, father.

Moon — emotions, feelings, reaction and response, memory, nurturance, changeability, belonging, the tribe, the public, women, mother.

Mercury — communication, navigation, logic, reason, dexterity, speech, writing, wit, cleverness, nervous system, siblings, neighbors.

Venus — attraction, love, affection, artistry, harmony, beauty, values, peace, art and decoration, females, relating, social interaction, social events.

Mars — action, drive, risk, initiative, aggressiveness, courage, desire, energy, passion, will, impulsiveness, force, competitiveness, males.

Jupiter — growth, expansiveness, optimism, law, religion, higher education, long journeys, justice, prosperity, generosity, confidence, extravagance, excess.

Saturn — limitation, restriction, boundaries, inhibition, delay, structure, caution, fear, control, ambition, responsibility, discipline, old age, father.

Uranus — deviation, eccentricity, sudden change, progress, rebellion, independence, division, liberation, originality, invention, technology.

Neptune — sensitivity, sacrifice, spirituality, escapism, illusion, deception, unification, vagueness, imagination, idealism, confusion, dreams, drugs, art/music, dancing, acting, film.

Pluto — deep change, crisis, transformation, regeneration, elimination, destruction, death, survival, compulsion, power, group resources, finance.

Dignities and Debilities

Traditionally the essential natures of the planets are considered more easily (or less easily) expressed in certain signs than in others. There are two types of dignities and debilities – essential and accidental. Essential dignities are those a planet receives based on its placement in a sign or segment of a sign. Accidental dignities are those based on house placement and aspects. The categories of essential dignity covered on Level I include:

Rulership—Planets are considered strongest in the signs they rule

Exaltation—Second strongest placement of a planet

Detriment—Found in the sign opposite its rulership and considered a weak placement for the planet

Fall—Found in the sign opposite its exaltation and considered the weakest placement for the planet

Table 1

SIGN	RULER	DETRIMENT	EXALTATION	FALL
ARIES	Mars	Venus	Sun	Saturn
TAURUS	Venus	Mars (Pluto)	Moon	
GEMINI	Mercury	Jupiter		
CANCER	Moon	Saturn	Jupiter	Mars
LEO	Sun	Saturn (Uranus)		
VIRGO	Mercury	Jupiter (Neptune)	Mercury	Venus
LIBRA	Venus	Mars	Saturn	Sun
SCORPIO	Mars (Pluto)	Venus	Mars	Moon
SAGITTARIUS	Jupiter	Mercury		
CAPRICORN	Saturn	Moon	Mars	Jupiter
AQUARIUS	Saturn (Uranus)	Sun		
PISCES	Jupiter (Neptune)	Mercury	Venus	Mercury

Table 1. Astrologers who practice Classical Astrology generally do not use the modern planets (Uranus, Neptune, and Pluto) as sign rulers. These planets were not known when the scheme of essential dignities was developed. In the table above, the proposed rulerships (or co-rulerships) of the modern planets, and also their logical detriment signs, are indicated in parentheses. Also, modern authors have proposed exhaltation and fall signs for the modern planets Uranus, Neptune and Pluto. Also, Mercury is thought to be exalted in Aquarius and in fall in Leo.

Benefics/Malefics

According to Classical Astrology, there are many ways of determining planetary qualities and strength. The following are the most general: Venus and Jupiter are considered benefic or fortunate planets; Mars and Saturn malefics or unfortunate planets. The Sun, Moon and Mercury are considered neutral.

Planetary Sect

Planetary sect divides the planets into diurnal and nocturnal categories. The diurnal planets are Sun, Jupiter, and Saturn; the nocturnal planets are Moon, Venus, and Mars. Mercury is diurnal if it rises before the Sun, nocturnal if it sets after the Sun. In a diurnal birthchart (Sun above the horizon), the diurnal planets have some advantage; in a nocturnal birthchart (Sun below the horizon), the nocturnal planets have some advantage. Also, diurnal planets prefer to be on the same side of the horizon as the Sun and in masculine (fire or air) signs; nocturnal planets prefer to be on the other side of the horizon as the Sun and in feminine (earth or water) signs.

Mutual Reception

Planetary strength may be enhanced through mutual reception, whereby two planets are in each other's signs of dignity and are thought to be in a position to help each other. This is especially the case if the two planets are in signs that aspect each other, or if a planet is dignified. For example: Sun in Aries and Mars in Leo (signs are in trine relationship; also Sun is in its exaltation). If one or both planets are also debilitated, such as Mercury in Sagittarius and Jupiter in Gemini, the benefits of mutual reception are weakened.

In Classical Astrology, a mutual reception could also happen between Planet A in the sign ruled by Planet B and Planet B in the sign in which Planet A is exalted; or between two planets in exaltation signs of the other. Examples are: Venus in Aries and Mars in Pisces; or Moon in Aries and Sun in Cancer; or Moon in Libra and Saturn in Taurus.

Retrogrades

The qualities of retrograde planets are internalized, reversed, or slower to develop. The Sun and Moon are never retrograde. See Figure 1, an illustration of retrograde motion in this study guide.

Signs of the Zodiac

The zodiac is the sky-band within which the Sun, Moon and planets move. There are 12 signs of the zodiac which symbolize a range of characteristics and modify the expression of the planets. There are two zodiacs in use in astrology: tropical (the signs) and sidereal (the constellations). In Western astrology the tropical zodiac is almost universally used and it is this zodiac that the Study Guide is concerned with. Note: Planetary rulerships of signs are given above in the section on dignities and debilities.

Glyphs

♈ — Aries   ♎ — Libra
♉ — Taurus   ♏ — Scorpio
♊ — Gemini   ♐ — Sagittarius
♋ — Cancer   ♑ — Capricorn
♌ — Leo   ♒ — Aquarius
♍ — Virgo   ♓ — Pisces

Keywords (behavioral)

The keywords given below apply, at minimum, to positions of the Sun, Moon and Ascendant in the signs. The signs also modify the nature of the planets, which is reflected in the traditional doctrine of essential dignities. Signs should be considered in terms of their element, polarity and quality (see below). For example, Aries is a fire sign, an active sign and a cardinal sign, all of which gives insight into the sign's basic nature.

Aries — active, direct, spontaneous, initiating, self-assertive, energetic, naive, "me first," ardent, leader.

Taurus — stable, persistent, sensual, materialistic, possessive, security-oriented, comfort-loving, patient, determined, stubborn, practical.

Gemini — restless, communicative, curious, versatile, flexible, quick-witted, diversified, scattered.

Cancer — sensitive, emotional, instinctual, sentimental, memory-retentive, nurturing, self-protective, family/mother/home-oriented.

Leo — warm-hearted, loyal, generous, dramatic, proud, regal, paternalistic, creative, dominating.

Virgo — discriminating, service-oriented, productive, health-conscious, technical, analytical, critical.

Libra — cooperative, partnership-oriented, social, appreciative of beauty, fair, balancing, indecisive, indolent.

Scorpio — intense, penetrating, secretive, jealous, introspective, passionate, strong-willed, possessive; urge for intimacy; death and regeneration.

Sagittarius — optimistic, enthusiastic, candid, speculative, adventurous, truth-seeking, philosophical, judgmental, tactless.

Capricorn — responsible, ambitious, organized, managerial, reserved, dutiful, cautious, somber, status seeking.

Aquarius — detached, humanitarian, individualistic, non-conforming, independent, aloof, impersonal.

Pisces — imaginative, self-sacrificing, impressionable, sympathetic, compassionate, illusionary, secretive, victimizing or victimized.

Elements (triplicities)

Fire — (Aries, Leo, Sagittarius) enthusiasm, zeal, warmth, idealism, creativity

Earth — (Taurus, Virgo, Capricorn) practicality, materialism, realism, concreteness

Air — (Gemini, Libra, Aquarius) mental activity, abstraction, communication, objectivity

Water — (Cancer, Scorpio, Pisces) emotions, intuition, compassion, subjectivity

Polarities

Active signs (positive – Fire and Air) are masculine, yang, initiating, extroverted

Receptive signs (negative – Earth and Water) are feminine, yin, responding, introverted

Qualities (modes / quadruplicities)

Cardinal — (Aries, Cancer, Libra, Capricorn) initiative and direct approach

Fixed — (Taurus, Leo, Scorpio, Aquarius) persistence and goal orientation

Mutable — (Gemini, Virgo, Sagittarius, Pisces) fluctuation, adaptability and social interaction

Houses

Houses (domiciles) are segments of the zodiac that are based on the timing of a birth or event. House positions of planets change by the hour as the Earth rotates. They represent categories, areas or departments of life that reflect, to some degree, the sequence of the zodiac.

Keywords

First house — physical body and overall health, personality, personal identity, beginnings, personal appearance.

Second house — ownership, material resources or possessions, physical senses, personal values, self-worth, talent, earning capacity.

Third house — communications, information exchange, mobility, early education, conscious mind, siblings, everyday ideas, neighbors and neighborhood, short trips.

Fourth house — home, territory, security, ancestry, real estate, foundations, family affairs, parent.*

Fifth house — creative self-expression, children, artistic production, speculation, sports, entertainment, love affairs, hobbies, pleasure-sharing friends.

Sixth house — daily work or routine, service, subordinates or employees, health issues and illness, small animals.

Seventh house — significant partnerships (marriage or business), one-to-one relationships, co-workers, consultants and consultations, lawsuits, open enemies or known opponents.

Eighth house — social bonding rituals and shared emotional experiences, other people's resources, financial entanglement, corporate finances, banking, debts, inheritance, taxes, death and regeneration, personal crises, surgery.

Ninth house — fundamental beliefs and assumptions, knowledge, philosophy, religion, higher education, law, wide distribution of information, distant travel.

Tenth house — public identity, social status and visibility, reputation, profession, career, employer, parent*, life-direction.

Eleventh house — peer group, like-minded friends, networks and like-minded groups, organizations, social equals, shared world view, shared hopes and wishes.

Twelfth house — Personal insight, confinement, activities behind the scenes, secret enemies, sanctuaries, spiritual growth, enlightenment, institutions, repression, the unconscious, self-undoing, large animals.

> *The assignment of one parent or the other to the fourth and tenth houses has varied over time and culture. In traditional Western astrology the fourth house is thought to signify the father, but can also be associated with the mother as per modern usage. The tenth house is thought to signify the mother traditionally, but can also be the father as per modern usage. This confusion is at least partly due to the rulerships of the fourth zodical sign Cancer and the tenth zodical sign Capricorn, which are associated with mother and father, respectively, and a real or perceived correspondence of these two signs with the fourth and tenth houses. The problem may be resolved to some extent by viewing the fourth house as signifying ancestral tradition which in Western societies is the source of the surname, which normally comes from the father. The tenth house may be viewed as signifying employers, managers and bosses, which is a role the mother, who mostly raises the child, has traditionally occupied in Western society. Of course, these roles can vary

according to cultural traditions and so the fourth and tenth houses may signify different things in different cultures and at different times in the history of cultures. For NCGR-PAA testing, the assignment of mother or father to the 4th or 10th houses can be based on either traditional or modern usage.

Quadrants

First quadrant — (houses 1, 2 and 3) self-development, self-worth, personal identity.

Second quadrant — (houses 4, 5 and 6) self-expression, creativity, adjustment to others.

Third quadrant — (houses 7, 8 and 9) awareness of others, social involvement.

Fourth quadrant — (houses 10, 11 and 12) integration with society, world consciousness.

Angularity

The **angular** houses are 1, 4, 7 and 10:

> First house — physical body
> Fourth house — emotional foundations
> Seventh house — significant others
> Tenth house — public identity

Note: Planets in angular houses have additional strength.

The **succedent** houses are 2, 5, 8, and 11:

> Second house — possessions
> Fifth house — creative desires
> Eighth house — merging instincts
> Eleventh house — peer group

The **cadent** houses are 3, 6, 9 and 12:

> Third house — conscious navigation of environment
> Sixth house — regulation of life processes
> Ninth house — understanding of the intellect
> Twelfth house — spiritual understanding

Interception

Interception occurs in certain house systems (e.g., Placidus) and more often at higher latitudes. With interception, one whole sign and parts of two others are in the same house. An intercepted sign never appears on the cusp of a house. If one sign is intercepted, its oppositional sign is also intercepted.

Derivation

The houses can also symbolize persons in the native's life derived by a special counting technique. For example, because the 7th house symbolizes the partner, the 8th house would represent the partner's 2nd house, and, therefore, can be used to investigate the partner's resources.

The Angles and the Nodes

The following are astronomical points (not physical bodies) generated from the intersection of planes that are typically employed in practical astrology. These are often categorized as personal points.

> **Ascendant** – identity, personality, physical appearance, self-perception.
> **Midheaven** – career, profession, honor, prestige, public perception by others.
> **Moon's Nodes** – social networks, connections, contacts.

Aspects

Aspects are the angular separations between two points as seen from the Earth, expressed in degrees. Some aspects are considered more powerful than others and have various qualities. The aspects most commonly used in practical astrology are based on division of the 360 degrees of the zodiac by whole numbers.

Conjunction (division of the circle by 1) 0° or 360°—Considered the most powerful aspect because of sign emphasis, but varying in meaning according to the planets involved

Opposition (division of the circle by 2) 180°—A polarity that shows a need to balance opposing forces. May be separative, or indicate enlightenment and awareness if integrated.

Trine (division of the circle by 3) 120°—A soft aspect, indicating a cooperative energy flow between two points.

Square (division of the circle by 4) 90°—A hard aspect, releasing tremendous energy which needs to be channeled and resolved. May be a building block or a stumbling block.

Sextile (division of the circle by 6) 60°—A soft aspect, offering opportunity or help from others.

Quincunx or Inconjunct (five-twelfths of the circle) 150°— Indicates strain and/or adjustment, sometimes related to health.

Semisextile (one-twelfth of the circle) 30°— In the same harmonic sequence as the quincunx, it indicates a minor strain or adjustment.

Semisquare (one-eighth of the circle) 45°— Similar to the square but less powerful.

Sesquisquare or Sesquiquadrate (three-eighths of the circle) 135°— Similar to the semisquare.

Aspects with their glyphs

☌ — Conjunction
⚺ — Semisextile
∠ — Semisquare
✶ — Sextile
□ — Square
△ — Trine
⚼ — Sesquisquare or Sesquiquadrate
⚻ — Quincunx or Inconjunct
☍ — Opposition:

Orbs

An orb is the arc (in degrees) within which an aspect is judged to be effective. There is some disagreement on the subject, so on tests, orbs to use will be indicated.

Aspects may be "in-sign" (e.g., Mars at 3° Aries trine Venus at 5° Leo); or aspects may be "out-of-sign" (e.g., Mars at 3° Aries trine Venus at 29° Cancer).

Aspects may be exact, applying or separating. An aspect is applying when the faster moving planet is at an earlier degree than the slower moving planet.

An aspect is separating when the faster moving planet is at a later degree than the slower moving planet.

Major Configurations

Stellium—Three or more planets in the same sign or house. A sign stellium indicates that the sign is strongly emphasized in the character of the native. A house stellium signifies an area of emphasis.

Grand Trine—Three planets 120° apart forming an equilateral triangle. The planets are ideally in the same element (fire, earth, air, or water). Possible easy flow of energy between the three planets, but can also indicate over-emphasis of the elements and planets involved.

Grand Cross—Two oppositions involving four planets in square to each other, ideally in the same mode (cardinal, fixed or mutable). Combines the definition of the square with the opposition. One of the most stressful configurations, but potentially creative. The individual must learn to mediate the energies to use them effectively.

T-square—Three planets of which two are in opposition and a third, focal planet is square both. Similar quality as the Grand Cross but less stressful, since the outlet for the stress is found in the house opposite the focal planet.

Grand Sextile—Six planets in sextile to each other in six different signs. This configuration does not occur frequently. It indicates emphasis of fire/air or earth/water. It also combines the qualities of the sextile, trine, and opposition. Often indicative of high achievement and dynamism.

Yod (Finger of God)—Two planets in sextile to each other and both quincunx a third, focal planet. It is mixed in effect and suggests tradeoffs, often involving a sacrifice.

Hemisphere and planetary distribution emphasis

East (left of the MC-IC axis) — one indication of an initiator

West (right of the MC-IC axis) — one indication of a responder

South (above the Ascendant-Descendant axis) — personal validity through interaction with the world; objective; extroverted energies

North (below the Ascendant-Descendant axis) — personal validity through interaction with the self; subjective; introverted energies

Quadrant emphasis (listed under Houses)

Jones Horoscopic Patterns or Distributions – Splay, Splash, Bundle, Bowl, Locomotive, Bucket, and Seesaw are categories that describe the fundamental tendencies of a chart.

Interpretation

The interpretation of a horoscope is a process of synthesizing and integrating the basic factors of astrology. The factors listed in this section (planets, angles, houses, signs, and aspects) are fundamental and must be mastered before adding more detail. In Level I, the student is expected to have knowledge of the basic components needed for interpretation and a general sense of how an interpretation might be accomplished. In Levels II, III, and IV more emphasis is placed on synthesis and interpretation.

Ethics (see Appendix I)

Interpreting horoscopes for other people is a serious endeavor and must be handled responsibly. Beginning students should mainly concentrate on learning the principles of astrology and applying these to general interpretation. Although one learns by interpreting charts for family and friends, the beginner must be cautious, and should avoid discussing critical or sensitive issues, unless he or she has had substantial prior training in counseling techniques. Avoid making any type of predictive statements at this Level, and take care to avoid any interpretive comment that may be psychologically damaging.

Keep in mind that there are always multiple things that can be said about any interpretive factor in astrology. Put yourself in the other's place. Often how something is said is much more important than what is said, in terms of how it is heard by the other. When you point out multiple options for how a factor in someone's chart might be interpreted and listen carefully to his/her feedback, you empower that person's personal ability and responsibility to choose, and open yourself to greater learning.

We highly recommend that anyone who aspires to be an

astrological consultant read and take seminars and courses in counseling techniques. Carefully read the NCGR-PAA Code of Ethics found in Appendix I. All candidates for NCGR-PAA testing on any and all Levels and all NCGR-PAA Certified Astrologers are expected to abide by this Code.

Calculations (see Appendix II)

The calculation of a horoscope is an exercise in simple algebra and geometry roughly equivalent to the high school level of education in mathematics. NCGR-PAA believes that knowledge of chart calculations provides a deeper understanding of the basis of a horoscope, something that may be missed entirely with complete dependence on computers. Students are required to calculate house cusps accurately within 30' of arc, the Moon within 15' of arc and all other planets within 5' of arc using any of the several methods available. Students should also be able to erect charts for both east and west longitudes, north and south latitudes.

Calculation Tools and References

- Ephemerides
- Tables of houses
- Reference books listing time zones and daylight time data
- Reference books listing longitudes and latitudes

Accuracy of Birth Data

We emphasize the importance of obtaining accurate birth data. Birth data may be obtained via services such as www.vitalchek.com. U.S. Government data on where to obtain or write for vital records is found from the Centers for Disease Control and Prevention website (www.cdc.gov). From this homepage a search for vital records will lead to information about obtaining state birth records. Knowledge of the time of birth is of extreme importance for astrological calculations and this data may or may not appear on a birth certificate. It is more likely to be shown on a hospital birth record, which is the document that should be requested. Accuracy of published birth data is also rated by the Rodden Rating System (see www.astro.com) and should be considered when interpreting the charts of public figures.

Categories of Time

- Sidereal Time
- Clock Time (Standard and Daylight Savings Time)
- Local Mean Time

Acceptable Methods for Calculations

- Direct (tables)
- Proportions (algebra)
- Trigonometry
- Logarithms

Acceptable Tools for Calculations

- Calculator (four function or scientific)
- Logarithmic tables
- Tables of Diurnal Motion

Astronomical Information

The Solar System

The solar system consists of a central star (the sun) and eight large bodies (planets) revolving around it. The inner planets (Mercury, Venus, Earth and Mars) are small, dense bodies collectively called the Terrestrial Planets and Jupiter, Saturn, Uranus and Neptune are large bodies, of mostly gases, called the Jovian Planets. The orbits of the planets around the sun are elliptical. The eight planets, in order of distance from the sun are: Mercury, Venus, Earth, Mars, Jupiter, Saturn, Uranus, and Neptune. In addition, there are two belts of smaller bodies, the asteroid belt located between the orbits of Mars and Jupiter, and the Kuiper belt located beyond Neptune. Ceres is the largest body in the asteroid belt and is classified by astronomers as a dwarf planet. Pluto is a Kuiper belt object and is also classified as a dwarf planet. Both of these are used extensively in astrology, as are many other objects orbiting in these belts. Most planets, including dwarf planet Pluto, have one or more satellites revolving around them. The moon is Earth's only natural satellite.

What is a planet? Regarding Solar System Objects
Used in Astrology

In August of 2006 the members of the International Astronomical Union voted on a new definition of a planet (www.iau.org). The winning criteria were:

1. The body must orbit a star.
2. It must have cleared its orbit of other bodies.
3. It must have enough mass to be nearly round.

According to these definitions, there are now eight planets in our solar system that are grouped into two sets. The first are the inner or terrestrial planets: Mercury, Venus, Earth, and Mars. These bodies are relatively small in size and are composed of rock and metals. The second are the outer or Jovian planets: Jupiter, Saturn, Uranus, and Neptune. These planets are very large and are made up of gases, liquids, and ice. Planets dominate their orbital zone. Moons, even the two that are larger than the planet Mercury, are seen as the property of the planet they orbit.

In addition to planets, the solar system is full of debris, pieces of rock and ice that have settled into orbits around the sun. Most of this debris is located in a belt between Mars and Jupiter called the Asteroid Belt. Here are found many large asteroids used by astrologers including Ceres, Pallas, Juno, and Vesta. A second debris belt found outside of the orbit of Neptune is called the Kuiper Belt and includes the planet Pluto, its moon Charon, and a number of other relatively large bodies that have only recently been discovered. Some of these

Kuiper Belt Objects (KBO's) are Makemake, Quaoar, and Eris— but there are many more. Astronomers realized they had a classification problem when the data available at that time suggested that Eris was larger than Pluto, and that Pluto, Eris, and Ceres were round. To resolve the problem a new term was coined: dwarf planets. There is also a category which can be described as Centaurs: escaped Kuiper Belt Objects such as Chiron (found between Saturn and Uranus) and other objects found within the territory of the Jovian planets.

The new definitions mentioned above are useful for astronomers who need to discriminate between bodies such as asteroids or comets, but they may not be useful for astrologers who would prefer to develop a planetary classification system based on observations of astrological effects. The NCGR-PAA certification program is concerned with knowledge of the sensitive points most frequently used by the majority of contemporary astrological researchers and practitioners. These do not always follow the classification boundaries established by astronomers. Further, terminology may differ as well. The use of the term planet has been applied to the Sun and Moon in astrology, although every astrologer knows they are not planets. Likewise, Pluto has become established as an important sensitive point by a majority of researchers and practitioners and is commonly referred to as a planet, regardless of the current definition. Although Ceres has been classified by astronomers as a dwarf planet, it is still commonly referred to in the astrological community as an asteroid.

Interestingly, it is not yet clear in the astronomical community whether dwarf planet status is, like planet status, a sole defining category, or whether dwarf planets also retain their previous minor body classifications, such as asteroid. It remains to be seen how astrological researchers and practitioners will refer to the Kuiper Belt Objects.

Note: At the present time, the NCGR-PAA exams will continue to respect the classification of Pluto as a planet and Ceres as an asteroid, while bearing in mind that astronomers have classified both of them as dwarf planets.

The View from Earth

Although the sun is the center of the solar system, we live on Earth and see the universe as revolving around us. This is known as an Earth-centered or geocentric view. From our viewpoint on Earth, the sun seems to travel around us once a day and moves through the background of stars once a year. In reality, this apparent motion of the sun is due to the motions of our own planet. One motion, called rotation, which accounts for the daily rising and setting of the sun, is simply the Earth spinning around a central axis, much like a toy top does. One complete turn takes approximately 24 hours or one day. The other motion, called revolution, the movement of Earth around the sun, accounts for the movement of the sun through the background stars. It takes 365.24 days, or one year, for one complete revolution.

The apparent path of the sun against the background of stars is called the ecliptic. All other planets as well as the moon move along this same path, although not always exactly on it. The zodiac is a band extending 8° on either side of the ecliptic through which most of the other bodies of the solar system pass. The projection of the Earth's equator into space is called the celestial equator. The plane of the ecliptic and the plane of the celestial equator intersect each other at an angle of 23.45°.

The zodiac is divided into twelve equal segments, each of which was named for the most prominent star group or constellation formerly seen within or approximately within that segment. These sections, which begin at the vernal equinox, became known as the signs of the tropical zodiac. About 2,000 years ago the signs of the tropical zodiac corresponded to the constellations for which they were named. Today, however, due to a process called precession of the equinoxes, the correspondence between the tropical sign and the constellation of the same name no longer exists. For example, today we find the tropical zodiac sign of Cancer in the section of the sidereal zodiac called Gemini.

The Seasons

Earth's axis is not straight up and down in relation to its orbit around the sun. Relative to the plane of the Earth's orbit, we would see that Earth tilts by 23.45°. This tilt, also found in the angle of intersection of the ecliptic and celestial equator, is responsible for the seasons. It is also responsible for the difference in the length of daylight during the seasons.

Solstices and Equinoxes

The solstices occur when the sun reaches its maximum distance (23.45°) north or south of the celestial equator. The vernal and autumnal equinoxes occur when the sun (always on the ecliptic) crosses the celestial equator. At the summer solstice (in the northern hemisphere) the sun reaches its maximum distance north of the celestial equator, and at the winter solstice the sun reaches its maximum distance south of the celestial equator. In the southern hemisphere, the seasonal effects of the solstices are reversed.

The vernal equinox correlates with the sun at 0° Aries and the autumnal equinox with the sun at 0° Libra. The sun reaches its maximum distance north of the equator when it is at 0° Cancer. This is the summer solstice and summer in the northern hemisphere. When the sun reaches its greatest distance south of the equator at 0° Capricorn it is the winter solstice and winter in the northern hemisphere.

Eclipses

There are two kinds of eclipses: solar and lunar. A solar eclipse occurs at the new moon when the moon passes between the sun and Earth, casting a shadow on Earth. A lunar eclipse occurs at the full moon, when Earth is between the sun and the moon, and the shadow of Earth falls on the moon. The 18-year Saros cycle is used to predict when eclipses will occur. From any given eclipse, another will occur in the same general part of zodiac 18 years later.

Retrograde Motion

Retrograde motion is an optical illusion. For a planet inside of Earth's orbit to appear retrograde, it must be passing in front of the sun:, that is, making a conjunction with the sun from the geocentric point of view. This is called an inferior conjunction. All planets outside Earth's orbit give the illusion that they are moving backward when Earth is between one of them and the sun. From the geocentric point of view, this is an opposition between the planet and the sun. In both cases retrogradation occurs when the planet is closest to Earth. The sun and the moon are the only bodies in our solar system that do not appear to move retrograde.

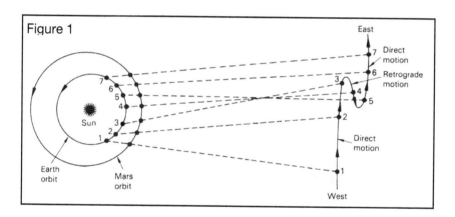

Figure 1. Illustration of the retrograde motion of Mars as seen from Earth. Earth orbits the Sun faster than Mars. The numbers of successive positions of Earth matched with the positions of Mars, and projected to celestial sphere, show the illusion of retrogradation. (history/NASA.gov)

Suggested Reading and References, Level I

Note: Books under the heading of one level are not repeated on successive levels. Assume that book recommendations are cumulative. Preparation for each level assumes familiarity with material from prior levels.

Although in many instances a book was originally published at an earlier date – especially some astrology classics – only the most recent publication date and publisher are listed, to facilitate finding titles online and in bookstores as per their present-day availability.

You can find books on this list, and those in the succeeding levels, including scarce and out-of-print books, through Internet searches of one or more of the following sites:

- www.allbookstores.com
- www.astrologyetal.com
- www.amazon.com
- www.half.com
- www.barnesandnoble.com
- www.powells.com

In the case of self-published titles, an information source is specified with the entry.

Introductory Texts

Arroyo, Stephen. *Astrology, Psychology, and the Four Elements: An Energy Approach to Astrology and Its Use in the Counseling Arts.* CRCS Publications. 1978.

Banzhaf, Hajo and Anna Haebler. *Key Words for Astrology.* Weiser Books. 1996.

Burk, Kevin. *Astrology: Understanding the Birth Chart.* Llewellyn. 2001.

Burt, Kathleen. *Archetypes of the Zodiac*. Llewellyn. 1988.

Davison, Ronald C. *Astrology: The Classic Guide to Under-standing Your Horoscope*. CRCS Publications. 1988.

Forrest, Steven. *The Inner Sky: How to Make Wiser Choices for a More Fulfilling Life*. Seven Paws Press. 2007.

Hone, Margaret E. *The Modern Text-Book of Astrology*. Astrology Classics. 2010.

Houlding, Deborah. *The Houses: Temples of the Sky*. The Wessex Astrologer. 2006.

Kempton-Smith, Debbi. *Secrets from a Stargazer's Notebook: Making Astrology Work for you*. Topquark. 1999

Levine, Joyce and Alphee Lavoie. *A Beginner's Guide to Astrological Interpretation*. Visualizations. 1995.

March, Marion D. and Joan McEvers. *The Only Way to Learn Astrology, Vol. 1: Basic Principles, 2nd edition*. ACS. 2008.

March, Marion D. and Joan McEvers. *The Only Way to Learn Astrology, Vol. 2: Math & Interpretation Techniques, 3rd edition*. Starcrafts Publishing. 2009.

Negus, Joan, *Basic Astrology: A Guide for Teachers and Students*. ACS. 1978.

Negus, Joan. *Cosmic Combinations: A Book of Astrological Exercises*. ACS. 1982.

Oken, Alan. *Alan Oken's Complete Astrology: The ClassicGuide to Modern Astrology*. Nicolas Hays, Inc. 2006.

Parker, Julia and Derek Parker. *Parker's Astrology: The Definitive Guide to Using Astrology in Every Aspect of Your Life.* Dorling Kindersley. 2001.

Pottenger, Maritha. *Easy Astrology Guide: How to Read Your Horoscope.* ACS. 1996.

Rogers-Gallagher, Kim. *Astrology for the Light Side of the Brain.* ACS. 2013.

Sasportas, Howard. *The Twelve Houses.* LSA/Flare. 2009.

Scofield, Bruce. *User's Guide to Astrology.* One Reed Publications. 1997.

Soffer, Shirley. *The Astrology Sourcebook: Your Guide to Understanding the Symbolic Language of the Stars, Revised edition.* Self-published. 2010. Available at www.amazon.com.

Reference: Dictionaries, Rulerships, and Encyclopedias

Bills, Rex E. *The Rulership Book.* AFA. 2007.

Brau, Jean-Louis, Helen Weaver, and Allan Edmonds, eds. *Larousse Encyclopedia of Astrology.* McGraw-Hill Book Company. 1992.

Carter, C.E.O. *An Encyclopaedia of Psychological Astrology.* Astrology Classics. 2005.

deVore, Nicholas. *Encyclopedia of Astrology.* Astrology Classics. 2005.

Gettings, Fred. *The Arkana Dictionary of Astrology.* Penguin Books. 1991.

Lehman, J. Lee, Ph.D. *Essential Dignities.* Whitford Press. 2013.

Lehman, J. Lee, Ph.D. *The Book of Rulerships: Keywords from Classical Astrology.* Whitford Press. 2000.

Lewis, James R. *The Astrology Book: The Encyclopedia of Heavenly Influences.* Visible Ink. 2003.

Munkasey, Michael. *Astrological Thesaurus, Book One: House Keywords.* Llewellyn. 1995.

Chart Collections

Rodden, Lois M. *Profiles of Women: Astro-Data.* Data Newz. 1996.

Rodden, Lois M. *Astro-Data 2: American Book of Charts.* AFA. 1984.

Rodden, Lois M. *Astro-Data III.* AFA. 1986.

Rodden, Lois M. *Astro-Data IV.* AFA. 1992.

Rodden, Lois M. *Astro-Data V: Profiles in Crime.* Data Newz. 1992.

Books Helpful for Interpretation

Barz, Ellynor. *Gods and Planets: The Archetypes of Astrology.* Chiron Publications. 1993.

Carter, C.E.O. *The Astrological Aspects.* AFA. 2000.

Dobyns, Zipporah. *Finding the Person in the Horoscope.* AFA. 2012.

George, Demetra. *Astrology and the Authentic Self: Integrating Traditional and Modern Astrology to Uncover the Essence of the Birth Chart.* Ibis Press. 2008.

Greene, Liz. *Saturn: A New Look at an Old Devil.* Red Wheel/Weiser. 2001.

Guttman, Ariel and Kenneth Johnson. *Mythic Astrology: Archetypal Powers in the Horoscope.* Llewellyn. 1998.

Hand, Robert. *Planets in Youth: Patterns of Early Development.* Schiffer Publishing. 1997.

Jayne, Vivia. *Aspects to Horoscope Angles.* AFA. 2014.

Jayne, Vivia. *By Your Lights.* AFA. 1986.

Jones, Marc Edmund. *Guide to Horoscope Interpretation.* Quest Books. 1981.

Levine, Joyce. *Breakthrough Astrology: Transform Yourself and Your World.* Weiser Books. 2006.

Lewi, Grant. *Astrology for the Millions.* Llewellyn. 2002.

Lewi, Grant. *Heaven Knows What.* Llewellyn. 2002.

Mann, A. T. *A New Vision of Astrology.* Gallery Books. 2002.

Marks, Tracy. *The Art of Chart Interpretation: A Step-by-Step Method for Analyzing, Synthesizing, and Understanding Birth Charts.* Ibis Press. 2008.

Marks, Tracy. *Planetary Aspects: From Conflict to Cooperation – How to Handle Your T-Square.* Ibis Press. 2014.

Rudhyar, Dane. *The Astrological Houses: The Spectrum of Individual Experience.* CRCS Publications. 1986.

Simms, Maria Kay. *Your Magical Child.* ACS. 1998.

Spiller, Jan. *Astrology for the Soul.* Bantam. 1997.

Stanley, Ena. *Archetypes of Astrology.* ACS. 2012.

Tierney, Bill. *The Dynamics of Aspect Analysis: New Perceptions in Astrology.* CRCS Publications. 1993.

Tompkins, Sue. *Aspects in Astrology: A Guide to Understanding Planetary Relationships in the Horoscope.* Destiny Books. 2002.

Van Toen, Donna. *The Astrologer's Node Book.* Red Wheel/Weiser. 1981.

Astronomy

Filbey, John and Peter Filbey. *Astronomy for Astrologers.* Aquarian Press. 1984.

Heath, Robin. *Sun, Moon and Earth.* Walker & Co. 2001.

Mayo, Jeff. *The Astrologer's Astronomical Handbook.* L. N. Fowler, Ltd. 1976.

Chart Calculations

Epstein, Meira B. *Excellence in Astrology: Preparation Material for Certification Exams, Level-I; Astronomy for Astrologers; Natal Chart Calculations; Astrology Fundamentals.* Available from Publisher Dr. Winai Ouypornprasert at iuf_6@yahoo.com. 2013.

Fowks, Lauran and Lynn Sellon. *Simply Math: A Comprehensive Guide to Easy & Accurate Chart Calculation.* Twelfth House Press. 2005.

Scofield, Bruce. *Astrological Chart Calculations: An Outline of Conventions and Methodology.* One Reed Publications. 2002.

Where to Write for Vital Records

Where to Write for Vital Records, U.S. Dept. of Health & Human Services, Center for Disease Control & Prevention. 2014. Available at www.amazon.com.

Where to Write for Vital Records: Births, Deaths, Marriages, & Divorces. Diane Publishing Co., 2007. Available at www.amazon.com.

Online source for data and charts: www.astro.com.

Online source for vital records: www.vitalchek.com.

Ephemerides

The American Ephemeris series, ACS/Starcraft Publishing. Originally compiled and programmed by Neil F. Michelsen, with updates on newer editions by Rique Pottenger.

The American Ephemeris for the 20th Century: 1900 to 2000 at Noon. ACS. 1994.

The American Ephemeris for the 20th Century: 1900 to 2000 at Midnight, 5th revised edition. ACS. 2000.

The New American Ephemeris for the 20th Century: 1900-2000 at Noon. Starcraft Publishing. 2009.

The New American Ephemeris for the 20th Century: 1900-2000 at Midnight. Starcraft Publishing. 2008.

The American Ephemeris for the 21st Century, (revised), Noon and Midnight versions. ACS. 1997.

The American Ephemeris for the 21st Century 2000-2050 at Noon. Starcraft Publishing. 2010.

The American Ephemeris for the 21st Century 2000-2050 at Midnight. Starcraft Publishing. 2010.

The New American Ephemeris for the 21st Century 2000-2100 at Midnight. Starcraft Publishing. 2006.

The New American Ephemeris 2007-2020: Longitude, Declination, Latitude and Daily Aspectarian. Starcraft Publishing. 2007.

The American Heliocentric Ephemeris, 2001-2050. Starcraft Publishing. 2007.

The American Sidereal Ephemeris, 2001-2025. Starcraft Publishing. 2007.

Tables of Planetary Phenomena, 3rd edition: ephemerides of numerous phenomena, such as eclipses, ingresses, planetary distances, stations, clusters, lunar phases, etc. Starcrafts Publishing, 2006.

Ephemerides: The Rosicrucian Ephemeris, 1900-2000, (Midnight). Rosicrucian Fellowship. 1993.

The Rosicrucian Ephemeris: 2000-2100, (Noon). Rosicrucian Fellowship. 1992.

The Astrolabe World Ephemeris, 2001-2050 at Noon. Whitford Press. 1998.

The Astrolabe World Ephemeris, 2001-2050 at Midnight: Featuring Longitudes & Declinations for the Sun, Moon, Planets, Chiron and the Asteroids. Schiffer Publishing. 2000.

Maynard, Jim. *The Pocket Astrologer.* Quicksilver Productions. Yearly publication.

Tables of Houses

The Michelsen Book of Tables, 2nd edition: Koch and Placidus Tables of Houses, How to Cast a Natal Horoscope, Interpolation Tables, Time Tables. ACS. 2009.

Tables of Houses: Placidus System. By Astro-Numeric Service. AFA. 2013.

Tables of Houses: Koch System. By Astro-Numeric Service. AFA. 1977.

Longitudes, Latitudes, and Time Changes

The American Atlas, Expanded Fifth Edition. Compiled and programmed by Thomas Shanks. ACS. 1996.

The International Atlas: World Longitudes & Latitudes, Time Changes and Time Zones, Expanded 6th Edition. Compiled and programmed by T. Shanks and R. Pottenger. ACS. 2005.

Study Guide for Level II

Review and expansion of core symbolism. Planetary cycles. Coordinate systems and the celestial sphere. House division. Transits, progressions and solar arc directions. Asteroids and fixed stars. Understanding of the material at this level should progress beyond keyword definitions toward interpretive synthesis.

Expansion of Core Symbolism

Ethics

See this section in the Level I Guide and carefully reread it and the NCGR-PAA Code of Ethics in Appendix I. As you begin to study forecasting techniques, keep in mind that the future is not fixed and there are multiple options at any point in time. In the test for this Level and beyond, questions involving consulting ethics will be included and will stress common sense and a positive, constructive approach.

Potential Uses of Chart Interpretation

1. Character analysis, event analysis.
2. Timing of events, either cyclic or for forecasting.
3. Answering specific questions; horary astrology.

Different Zodiacal Systems

Tropical

Utilizes a zodiac that is tied to the seasonal cycle, and begins with the vernal equinox that establishes 0° Aries. This zodiac is used by the vast majority of astrologers in Western countries.

Sidereal

Utilizes a zodiac based upon the constellations of fixed stars which coincided with the signs of the tropical zodiac about 2000 years ago. The sidereal zodiac moves backward through the tropical zodiac at the rate of approximately 50 seconds per year or 1 degree every 72 years. This motion is known as precession. The sidereal zodiac is not definitively anchored to a single point in the constellations and a number of versions exist. Sidereal zodiacs are used by Hindu/Vedic astrologers and astrologers in the West called Siderealists.

Planets

Mutual Reception

See Level I Guide for review. Two planets in mutual reception are interpreted as working together as a unit – regardless of any aspect, or lack of aspect, between them.

Dispositor

Ruler of the sign in which another planet is placed. For example, if Mars is in Libra, Venus (ruler of Libra) is said to be the dispositor of Mars. The driving energy of Mars is thus softened by Venus and Libra.

Final Dispositor

In some charts, a chain of dispositors is formed, where one planet is said to be the final dispositor of all other planets in the chart, since all the other planets ultimately disposit to it. To qualify as a final dispositor, a planet (and only one planet) must be in a sign it rules or co-rules. At least one other planet must also be in that same sign or in the sign the final dispositor planet co-rules. The final dispositor signifies strong and important themes in a person's life.

Decanates

Decans are 10° sections of a sign. The concept probably originated in Egypt where the risings of specific stars on the horizon at 10 degree intervals was used for time-keeping purposes. This idea was used in Greek and Indian astrology and there are several versions of rulership orders. In Classical Astrology 10° sections are called Faces. Although the 30° span of a sign encompasses a full sign, the most popular decanate theory currently holds that the first 10° of each sign most strongly represent the qualities of that sign; the next 10° of that sign include qualities of the next sign in the same triplicity; and the final 10° include qualities of the third sign in that triplicity. For example, the first 10° of Aries represent the qualities of Aries most, the second 10° of Aries include Leonine qualities, and the final 10° of Aries include Sagittarian qualities.

Minor Aspects

All aspects result from the division of the 360° circle by whole numbers. For example, the trine (120°) is obtained by dividing 360° by 3. Minor aspects result from the division of the circle as follows:

- Divisor of 5: Quintile Series (72°, 144°)

- Divisor of 7: Septile Series (51.43°, 102.86°, 154.29°)

- Divisor of 8: Semisquare/Sesquiquadrate (45°, 135°)

- Divisor of 9: Nonile Series (40°, 80°, 160°)

- Divisor of 12: Semisextile/Quincunx (30°, 150°)

- Divisor of 16: Semioctile Series (22.5°, 67.5°, 112.5°, 157.5°)

Derived House Analysis

Particular houses in the natal chart can be used to evaluate situations concerning any number of other people.

Example: To find one's brother's wife's sister in the horoscope, the 3rd house describes the brother. In derived house analysis, it is considered the brother's 1st house; the 9th house would then represent the brother's wife (7th house from the 3rd). The 9th house also then becomes the wife's 1st house. The wife's sister is then the 11th house of the chart (3rd house from the 9th).

Synodic Cycles: Lunar and Planetary Phases Theory

A synodic cycle is a cycle between any two bodies, from conjunction through opposition and back to conjunction. The synodic cycle of the Moon and Sun is familiar and found on most calendars. Lunar phases are the angular distances between the Sun and the faster-moving Moon. An 8-phase model has ancient origins and was popularized in the 20th century by Dane Rudhyar. This model could be applied to any synodic cycle.

1. New Moon — 0° to 45° — birth, emergence, new beginning, projection of new direction

2. Crescent — 45° to 90° — expansion, struggle, crystallization of ideas or direction

3. First Quarter — 90° to 135° — crisis of action, expression and activation of ideas

4. Gibbous — 135° to 180° — analysis and evaluation, overcoming of obstacles

5. Full Moon — 180° to 225° (or to closing sesquiquadrate) — culmination, fulfillment, perfect realization

6. Disseminating — 225° to 270° (or to closing square) — demonstration and performance, distribution

7. Last quarter — 270° to 315° (or to closing semisquare) — crisis of consciousness

8. Balsamic — 315° to 360° (or closing semisquare to conjunction) — release of the past, preparation for and commitment to the future

Planets have the same phase relationships to each other as in the lunar phases. Substitute the slower moving planet for the Sun, and the faster moving planet for the Moon. For example, Mars at 5° Cancer is in its First Quarter phase to Saturn at 5° Aries. Interpretation is similar to that of lunar phases, i.e., it implies a crisis or a need to manage action.

Orbital Planetary Cycles

Approximate planetary cycles are:

Sidereal Cycle	Synodic Cycle (with Sun)
Mercury – 88 days	118 days
Venus – 224 days	584 days
Mars – 2 years	780 days
Jupiter – 12 years	399 days
Saturn – 29 years	378 days
Uranus – 84 years	370 days
Neptune – 165 years	367 days
Pluto – 245 years	367 days

For the synodic cycle (planetary position relative to the Sun), Mercury is never more than 28° from the Sun; Venus is never more than 48° from the Sun. The synodic periods of the outer planets are close to that of an Earth year because of their slow movement.

NCGR-PAA Study Guide

Coordinate systems and the Celestial Sphere

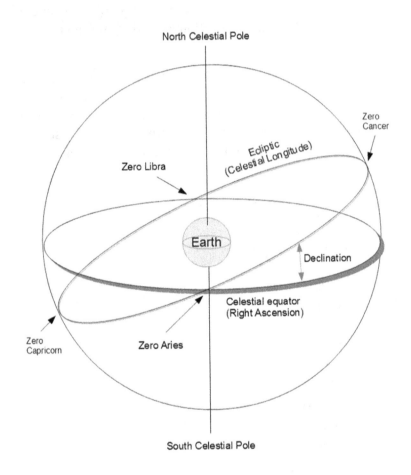

Figure 2. The Celestial Sphere. The projection of the Earth's equator and pole seen as the celestial equator and celestial poles. The ecliptic, or path of the Sun, is tilted to the equator by 23.45°. Where the equator and ecliptic intersect are the equinoxes. (from Scofield, Astrological Chart Calculations)

Great Circles

A great circle is defined as any circle, the plane of which passes through the center of a sphere (a sphere is the three-dimensional equivalent of a circle). A circle is defined as having all of its points equidistant from the center point of a plane, while a sphere has all points equidistant from a center point in a space. The celestial sphere is an imaginary sphere of infinite radius surrounding Earth (the terrestrial sphere) and serving as a screen against which we see all celestial objects. In this way positions of celestial objects can be mapped.

Horizon

The boundary between Earth and sky from an observer on the surface of the Earth. The celestial horizon is the plane parallel to the horizon but passing through the center of the Earth. Points on the horizon are designated in reference to the four compass points (north, east, south, and west). The zenith is the point directly above the observer, the nadir is the point directly below. These two points are poles of the celestial horizon.

Meridian

The meridian is a great circle passing through the observer's zenith, the south point of the horizon, the observer's nadir, the north point of the horizon, and back to the zenith. This circle divides Earth equally, east and west.

Prime Vertical

The Prime Vertical is a great circle passing through the observer's zenith, the east point of the horizon, the observer's nadir, the west point of the horizon, and back to the zenith. The prime vertical and the meridian intersect at the zenith and nadir.

Celestial Equator

The celestial equator is the Earth's equator extended into space. The poles of the equator (the actual poles of the rotating Earth) are at right angles (90°) to this plane.

Ecliptic

The ecliptic is a great circle created by the plane of Earth's orbit onto the celestial sphere. To an observer on the Earth, the ecliptic is the sun's apparent path around Earth.

Figure 3*

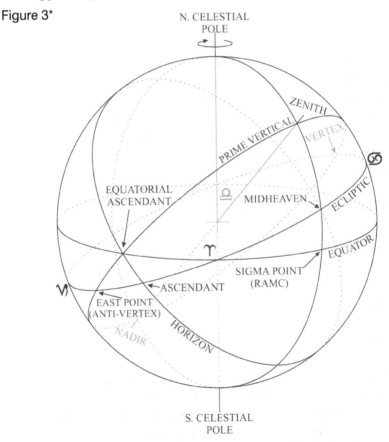

Figure 3. Celestial sphere showing equator, ecliptic, horizon and their major intersection points.

*© 1995, 1998, 2004, 2010, 2014 Gary Christen. Reprinted with Permission.

Other Astronomical Terms

Celestial Longitude

Distance measured along the ecliptic, in degrees, minutes and seconds, from the vernal equinox (0° Aries). Celestial longitude totals 360°, but is normally divided into twelve 30° sections (the signs).

Celestial Latitude

The distance, measured in degrees, minutes and seconds, of a stellar body north or south of the ecliptic. Celestial latitude ranges from 0° at the ecliptic to 90° at the poles of the ecliptic.

Right Ascension

The measurement eastward along the celestial equator from 0° Aries. Analagous to longitude on the terrestrial sphere. Right Ascension tracks the rotation of the Earth and is normally measured in hours and minutes.

Declination

The distance of a stellar body north or south of the celestial equator, measured in degrees, minutes and seconds. Declination is analagous to latitude on the terrestrial sphere and ranges from 0° at the equator to 90° at the poles.

Equinox

One of the two points created by the intersection of the ecliptic and the celestial equator. The vernal equinox is both 0° longitude and 0° latitude. The sun, always on the ecliptic, crosses the equator about March 21 each year. The autumnal equinox is 180° longitude and marks the opposite point on the ecliptic, where the sun crosses the equator about September 22.

Solstice

One of the two places where the sun attains its greatest declination, these points being halfway between the equinoxes. The summer solstice is the point on the ecliptic (at longitude 90°) where the sun is at its maximum northern declination (+23°27'); the winter solstice is the point on the ecliptic (at longitude 270°) where the sun is at its maximum southern declination (-23°27').

Cardinal Points

The equinox and solstice points on the ecliptic -i.e., 0° Aries, Libra, Cancer, and Capricorn.

Precession

The retrogression of the vernal point along the fixed (i.e., sidereal) ecliptic at the rate of about 50 arc seconds per year, or 1° every 72 years. About 2,160 years must pass to move 30° of celestial longitude; and about 26,000 years must pass to move 360° of celestial longitude.

Lunar Nodes

The degrees of intersection where the plane of the moon's orbit crosses the plane of the ecliptic. The point at which the moon crosses the ecliptic from south to north is called the North Node. The opposite point is called the South Node. The mean, or average Node travels backward in the zodiac at a uniform rate of approximately 3 minutes (3') of arc per day. True Node positions are based on the fact that the moon's orbital plane wobbles. The True Node position can vary from the Mean Node by up to 1°45'.

Planetary Nodes

Degrees where orbital planes of the planets intersect Earth's orbital plane.

Parallels and Contraparallels

These are "aspects" of declination. Two bodies are considered to be parallel if they are in the same degree of declination, and both are either north or south of the celestial equator.

Example: Mars at 11°S08' and Jupiter at 11°S08' are in parallel.

Example: Mars at 11°N08' and Jupiter at 11°S08' are contraparallel because they are in similar degrees of opposite declination.

Most authorities allow a maximum of a 1° orb of aspect and consider parallels to have a quality similar to that of a conjunction, while contraparallels operate similarly to an opposition.

Vertex and Equatorial Ascendant

Vertex

The intersection of the prime vertical and the ecliptic in the west. Thought by researchers to pertain to matters of fate. The vertex is the Ascendant at the co-latitude.

Equatorial Ascendant

The degree of the zodiac that would be rising if one were born at the equator. It is found by interpolating the Ascendant at 0° of latitude according to the correction of a given MC. Sometimes erroneously called the East Point.

Relocation Charts

When a person moves geographically, that person's natal chart will differ from one calculated for the new location. This can often be sensed intuitively because he or she will feel better in one place than in another. This difference can be evaluated for different locations anywhere in the world by comparing where the planets fall on the four angles of the chart as well as other factors.

To evaluate the conditions of a specific location, a relocated chart can be erected. This is done by recalculating the birthchart, using the new location and the equivalent time of birth based on the new location. The house cusps of the relocated chart will change, but the zodiacal positions of the planets remain the same.

Mundane Charts

Ingress charts

The entry of any orbital body into a sign is termed an ingress chart. The most commonly used ingress charts are those of the Sun entering the cardinal signs. A chart cast for the moment the Sun enters 0° Aries signifies the beginning of the astrological new year. Mundane astrologers typically use the Aries ingress chart, set for the location of the capital of a country or for any specific place in which they are interested, as a basis for analysis and interpretation. The chart is used to prognosticate governmental issues, social conditions, weather, etc. for the year ahead. Charts for 0° of the other cardinal signs are also used for prognosis of the affairs of each season, or quarter of the year.

Eclipses

A chart is cast for the exact time of a lunar or solar eclipse for a specific location. There is a difference of opinion as to the length of time during which the influence of an eclipse is felt.

Lunations

Charts cast for specified locations for the new Moon are read for prognosis of the trends for the month. Charts cast for the full Moon are read for the culmination of what began at the new Moon, or for the trends of the two-week period until the next new Moon.

Planetary Conjunctions

Frequently studied in terms of world trends and the destinies of nations and of large groups of people. These charts are cast for the time of a major cyclic aspect, such as the Jupiter-Saturn conjunction.

House Division

There are a number of ways to divide the sphere into the twelve parts astrologers refer to as houses. There is also a good deal of controversy over which particular system of house division is the best and how much it matters in interpreting a chart. Proponents of a specific system argue that the matter of house division is of great importance; however, the proof that one system is superior to another has never been shown. Nevertheless, most astrologers would agree that defining intermediate houses in some fashion is necessary.

Over the past century, the Placidus system has been the most widely used, but that is due to the fact that the Placidian tables were the easiest and least expensive to acquire. Now, however, Koch and other systems of house division are just as accessible through print or computer programs.

Quadrant Systems

Quadrant house systems are built around the longitudes of the Ascendant and Midheaven. All quadrant systems calculate the Ascendant and Midheaven in the same way. The difference among the various systems lies in the method by which the span of the ecliptic is divided by the angles of the chart.

Space-based quadrant systems

Porphyry

Porphyry is the first known quadrant system. This spatial method trisects all the quadrants between the four angles of the chart on the ecliptic, so that the succedent houses are 1/3rd of the distance from angle to angle, and the cadent houses are 2/3rds of the distance.

Campanus

The prime vertical is divided into twelve equal arcs by lunes (vertical sections of the sphere) whose poles are the north and south points of the horizon. Where the lunes cut the ecliptic are the house cusps. The arcs comprising the lunes are house semicircles.

Regiomontanus

The celestial equator is divided into twelve equal segments beginning at the east point. The house cusps are formed by the intersections of the house semi-circles with the ecliptic. Since the equator is not perpendicular to the north point-south point axis of the horizon, the houses are not equal.

Time-based quadrant systems

Systems based on time are distinguished from the systems based on space. However, all the time-based systems translate time into house cusps on the ecliptic. The general principle for these systems remains the same: the time of the semi-arc (movement from one angle to another) of some major mundane sensitive point is trisected, and that trisection becomes the basis for the house division.

Alcabitius

This ancient system of house division was very popular in the Middle Ages but probably originated during Roman times. It has been referred to as the "standard method." The Alcabitius system first calculates the sidereal time needed for the degree of the Ascendant to rotate to the Midheaven. This amount of sidereal time is then divided by three and the result is added to the sidereal time at birth in two installments to locate the eleventh and twelfth houses. A similar procedure is used to generate the second and third houses.

Study Guide for Level II

FIGURE 4a
Campanus Method

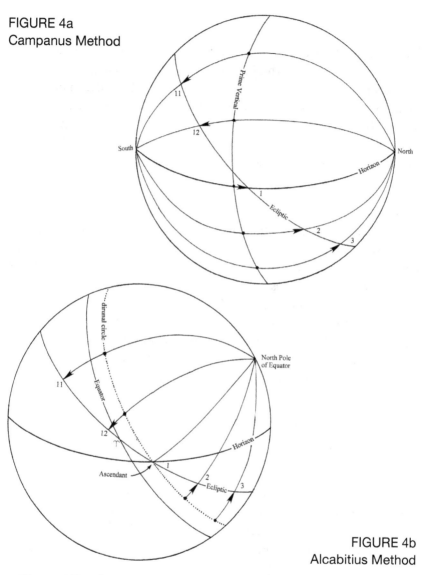

FIGURE 4b
Alcabitius Method

Figure 4 Two house systems. In the spatial Campanus system (4a) the east-west arc above the Earth, the prime vertical, is divided in equal segments and projected to the ecliptic to denote the house cusps. In the time-based Alcabitius system (4b) the rotation of the Earth on its axis is used as a measure. The time taken for rotation to bring a degree of the zodiac from the horizon to the Midheaven is trisected to produce house cusps.

Image from Scofield, Astrological Chart Calculations

Placidus

Each degree of the zodiac has a particular rate of movement as it rises from the Ascendant to the Midheaven, and also as it passes through the other three quadrants. The trisections of these diurnal or nocturnal semi-arcs establish the intermediate house cusps. Curves are formed by points each of which trisects its own diurnal or nocturnal semi-arc. Where these complex curves cross the ecliptic determine the cusps given in the Placidian tables of houses.

Koch

The diurnal semi-arc of the MC is trisected. Calling the trisections of the semi-arc X, the MC is then rotated backwards through its diurnal semi-arc. At this point the MC comes to the horizon. Then the MC is rotated X degrees off the horizon. The new Ascendant is the 11th house cusp. Rotating the MC another X degrees brings the 12th house cusp to the Ascendant, another X degrees being the 1st house cusp (the final Ascendant) to the Ascendant, another X degrees brings the 2nd house cusp to the Ascendant, and finally another X degrees brings the 3rd house cusp to the Ascendant.

An Alternative House System

The Meridian System

Meridian (or equatorial houses) is not technically a quadrant system because the Ascendant is not included in the calculation of the intermediate house cusps. The celestial equator is divided into twelve equal arcs by lunes from the poles of the celestial equator. The intersections of lunes with the ecliptic are considered the house cusps. Each house is exactly two sidereal hours long. The MC is the cusp of the 10th house and the equatorial ascendant is the cusp of the 1st house.

Zodiac-based House Systems

In addition to Alcabitius and Porphyry, the following house systems, each of which divides the zodiac evenly to create the twelve houses, were used in Hellenistic and Medieval astrology. These systems are used by some modern Western and Vedic astrologers.

Whole Sign

According to the whole sign house method, the 1st house begins at 0° of the sign of the Ascendant, and the remaining houses are signs of the zodiac following the sign of the 1st house. For example, in a chart with 5° Scorpio rising, all of Scorpio is always the 1st house, Aries is the 6th house, and Virgo the 11th house. In this system, neither the Ascendant nor the Midheaven are necessarily house cusps. Some astrologers are also now using Whole Sign houses in their division of the chart, though this method is not accepted on NCGR-PAA exams.

Equal House

The equal house system uses the degree of the Ascendant as the 1st house cusp, and the remaining houses are exactly 30° from the Ascendant degree, so that, in the above example of a 5° Scorpio rising, the 6th house cusp is 5° Aries, the 11th house cusp is 5° Virgo. Although the Ascendant is the 1st house cusp, the Midheaven is not necessarily the 10th house cusp. Some astrologers are also now using Equal houses in their division of the chart, though this method is not accepted on NCGR-PAA exams.

Planetary Rulerships and Disposition

Essential Dignity

Essential dignity shows how much a planet has hegemony due to its placement in the sign and degree of the zodiac. For example, using Saturn at 3° Libra in a day chart:

Venus is the sign ruler, Saturn the exaltation, Moon is the face ruler. Saturn is the triplicity ruler for a diurnal chart ("D" stands for "day" in Table 2 – *next page*). Saturn is also the term ruler for the first several degrees of Libra. According to tradition, Saturn here would be very highly dignified, even though it is not the sign ruler.

Table 2

A Table of the Essential Dignities of the PLANETS according to Ptolemy

Sign	Houses of the Planets	Exalt-ation	Triplicity of Planets		The Terms of the Planets					The Faces of the Planets			Detri ment	Fall
			D	N										
♈	♂ D	☉ 19	☉	♃	♃ 6	♀ 14	☿ 21	♂ 26	♄ 30	♂ 10	☉ 20	♀ 30	♀	♄
♉	♀ N	☽ 3	♀	☽	♀ 8	☿ 15	♃ 22	♄ 26	♂ 30	☿ 10	☽ 20	♄ 30	♂	
♊	☿ D	☊ 3	♄	☿	☿ 7	♃ 13	♀ 21	♄ 25	♂ 30	♃ 10	♂ 20	☉ 30	♃	
♋	☽ D/N	♃ 15	♂	♂	♂ 6	♃ 13	☿ 20	♀ 27	♄ 30	♀ 10	☿ 20	☽ 30	♄	♂
♌	☉ D/N		☉	♃	♄ 6	☿ 13	♀ 19	♃ 25	♂ 30	♄ 10	♃ 20	♂ 30	♄	
♍	☿ N	☿ 15	♀	☽	☿ 7	♀ 13	♃ 18	♄ 24	♂ 30	☉ 10	♀ 20	☿ 30	♃	♀
♎	♀ D	♄ 21	♄	☿	♄ 6	♀ 11	♃ 19	☿ 24	♂ 30	☽ 10	♄ 20	♃ 30	♂	☉
♏	♂ N		♂	♂	♂ 6	♃ 14	♀ 21	☿ 27	♄ 30	♂ 10	☉ 20	♀ 30	♀	☽
♐	♃ D	☋ 3	☉	♃	♃ 8	♀ 14	☿ 19	♄ 25	♂ 30	☿ 10	☽ 20	♄ 30	☿	
♑	♄ N	♂ 28	♀	☽	♀ 6	☿ 12	♃ 19	♂ 25	♄ 30	♃ 10	♂ 20	☉ 30	☽	♃
♒	♄ D		♄	☿	♄ 6	☿ 12	♀ 20	♃ 25	♂ 30	♀ 10	☿ 20	☽ 30	☉	
♓	♃ N	♀ 27	♂	♂	♀ 8	♃ 14	☿ 20	♂ 26	♄ 30	♄ 10	♃ 20	♂ 30	☿	☿

Table 2. The Table of Essential Dignities. *This traditional table gives the Classical determination of planetary rulerships and dispositions. The five-dignity system, which has its origins in Hellenistic astrology, is used by traditional astrologers in horary as well as natal astrology. The five dignities are rulership, exaltation, triplicity, term and face.*

Essential dignity can be quantified by assigning five points to sign ruler, four to exaltation, three to triplicity, two to term, and one to face. Detriment would get minus five, fall minus four, and planets without any essential dignity (peregrine) minus five. Thus, Saturn would get nine points at 3° Libra.

Accidental Dignity

Planets may have strength without being positioned in one or more of the categories of essential dignity. Traditional listings of accidental dignity point to considerations of angularity (location in the tenth, first, seventh and fourth houses), direction and motion, visibility, proximity to the Sun, increasing in light, aspects to other planets or the Part of Fortune, and conjunction with a fixed star of a fortunate nature. For example, accidentally dignified planets may be in the 1st or 10th houses, have trines from Venus or Jupiter, or be moving at maximum speed. There are other categories for accidental dignity as well, though these are the primary ones according to most traditional sources. One modern notion is that planets in houses that correspond with their rulership (i.e. Sun in the fifth house, Mercury in the third, etc.) have accidental dignity. Strong accidental dignity is thought to compensate for lack of essential dignity in certain ways; negatively it can emphasize the problems inherent in a planet's lack of essential dignity. Some traditional sources, notably William Lilly, have a point system for accidental dignity.

Almuten

The almuten, meaning overlord or dominator, is the most influential planet in a chart, its strength being determined by its essential dignities. In identifying the almuten the full range of the essential dignities must be considered and this is often done with a point scoring system.

Dynamic Techniques

Earliest Predictive Techniques

The ancients used a version of directions, known as primary directions, in which planets and other points were moved a very small amount per year based on the diurnal cycle of the day of one's birth.

Planetary period or chronocrator (time-lord) systems were also used. This system places specific planets as "rulers" for multiyear periods in a person's life, within which shorter terms are co-ruled by other planets. In this general category are the decennials of Hellenistic astrology which take the total time periods of the chronocrators, which is 129, and divides this by 10 creating a standard schemata. The Medieval firdaria are similar in that they also demarcate standard periods of time ruled by each of the planets and the Moon's node.

Profections are another Hellenistic technique in which horoscope emphasis advances one sign per year for a yearly ruler and one sign per month for a monthly ruler. This system may also include daily planetary rulers.

Solar returns (called "revolutions" by Lilly) have been used continuously from Hellenistic times up to the present day. Transits were of some small importance in ancient Western astrology but were considered most potent around the time of the solar return.

Transits

Transits should be thoroughly studied at Level II. Students should know the length of each planetary cycle (see Planetary Cycles in this study guide). Special emphasis should be placed on the timing and meaning of hard aspects (conjunctions, squares and oppositions) made by outer planets (Jupiter through Pluto) to their natal positions. Testing will likely include questions about simple interpretation of transit effects, transits as triggers, and generational themes of outer planet transits. Students should also familiarize themselves with transit tracking (i.e., following transits in the ephemeris).

Secondary Progressions

One day of actual planetary motion in the ephemeris is symbolically representative of one year in a person's life.

The ACD (Adjusted Calculation Date, or Limiting Date) is the starting date during the year on which the secondary progressions begin. It is the day on which the planetary positions in the ephemeris are accurate as given, without any interpolation. Level II testing requires the calculation of secondary progressions according to the ACD method.

Progressed Moon

Testing will require accurate calculations for the monthly movement of the progressed Moon. The approximate motion of the progressed Moon is 1° a month.

Declinations

Students must be able to list declinations for the progressed chart for the ACD.

Progressed House Cusps

The progressed MC can be calculated by the following methods. Note: the progressed Ascendant and other progressed house cusps are interpolated from the progressed MC using a table of houses.

Solar Arc. Find the difference between the progressed Sun and the natal Sun. Add the result to the natal MC for the position of the progressed MC on the ACD.

Mean Sidereal. Calculate a chart for the progressed date, using the natal time of birth.

Meridian Arc. Add 1° for each year of age to the natal MC.

Solar Arc Directions

Planets and other points are directed according to the arc of the Sun (progressed Sun minus the natal Sun).

To calculate the Solar Arc, subtract the position of the natal Sun from the position of the progressed Sun as given in the ephemeris for the ACD. This will give you the Solar Arc for the ACD.

To calculate the Solar Arc for a particular age, count forward in the ephemeris one day for each year of age, starting with the birthday.

From the ephemeris position of the Sun on the resulting day, subtract the ephemeris position of the Sun that is given on the birthday (not the natal Sun position). The result is the Solar Arc for the age in question, on the birthday.

Antiscia (or solstice points) Singular: antiscion

Defined as the reflective position or mirror image of a given planetary position with Cancer-Capricorn as the central axis. For example, the antiscion of 2° Cancer is 28° Gemini, and the antiscion of 3° Cancer is 27° Gemini, and so on.

The pairs of signs that reflect each other in this manner are as follows:

> Gemini-Cancer
> Taurus-Leo
> Aries-Virgo
> Pisces-Libra
> Aquarius-Scorpio
> Capricorn-Sagittarius

The Asteroids and Chiron

Asteroids in common usage are Ceres, Pallas Athene, Vesta, and Juno. These four, and many others used by astrologers, orbit in the asteroid belt located between the orbits of Mars and Jupiter. Chiron, which orbits between Saturn and Uranus, is one of many orbiting bodies classified as centaurs. These small solar system bodies, with characteristics of both asteroids and comets, have eccentric orbits located between the orbits of Jupiter and Neptune.

Ceres (mother)—Physical nurturing, food, grain, cooking, productivity, fertility, gardening, rural life.

Pallas Athene (father's daughter)—Warrior maiden, wisdom, justice, patterns, weaving, crafts, resourcefulness, industry (work), urban life, cultural institutions.

Vesta (sister)—Hearth and home, clannishness, safety and security, chastity, maiden aunt, vows, ritual duties.

Juno (married woman)—Wife, charm, adornment, cosmetics, fashion, jealousy, victim/victimizer, relating.

Chiron (centaur)—Wounded healer, mentor, primordial wisdom, high culture, ecology, traditional and alternative medicine, rape or violation, outcast, music, alternative education, stringed instruments.

Fixed Stars

Fixed stars precess in the heavens due to the very slow wobble of the poles. The rate of change is roughly 1 degree per 72 years. The positions given below are for the year 2014 (from Solar Fire software).

Algol, 26° Taurus 22' — Violence, misfortune, losing one's head, suffocation, fires, artistry, music, crisis, throat ailments, neck injuries.

Alcyone, 0° Gemini 12' — Largest of the Pleiades, ambitions, prominence, optimism, eye problems, star of sorrow, exile, banishment, weeping.

Aldebaran, 10° Gemini 00' — Royal Star, courage, power, honor, popular but embattled, notoriety, intelligence, heavy losses.

Sirius, 14° Cancer 17' — Brightest star, fame, riches, domestic problems, occult interests, inner vision, intense imagery, calendar star, dog bites, custodial duties, guardianship.

Castor, 20° Cancer 27' — Keen intellect, sudden rise and honors followed by fall, distinction, hypersensitive, fondness for horses, mischievousness, intemperance, aggressiveness.

South Asellus, 8° Leo 55' — Sudden downfalls, loss of reputation, seeking applause, domestic problems, hearing, speech, and mental problems, disappointments, fires, fevers, ghosts, UFOs.

Regulus, 0° Virgo 02' — Royal Star, honors, power, success, strong character, well-connected, ability to command, scandal, accidents.

Vindemiatrix, 10° Libra 08' — Star of widowhood, cautious, inner drive for recognition, fear of poverty or failure, worry, depression, materialistic, hypocritical.

Spica, 24° Libra 03' — good fortune, potential for brilliance, extraordinary talent, gifted, insight, honor, fame.

Arcturus, 24° Libra 26' — Renown, self-determination, prosperity, success through slow and patient work, belligerent, quarrelsome.

South Scale ((Zuben Elgenubi) - 15° Scorpio 17' — Karmic debt, betrayals, loss of relatives, unforgiving, untruthful, ability to overcome hardships, clever, hidden streak of cruelty.

North Scale (Zubenelschamali) - 19° Scorpio 35' — Star of fortune, high ambition, riches, enthusiastic, legal problems, organizational ability, highs and lows.

Antares, 9° Sagittarius 58' — Royal Star, great power, authority, headstrong, obstinate, gain through hard work, issues of racial and religious tolerance and human rights, suspicious, pugnacious, fires, nuclear events, exactly opposite Aldebaran.

Fomalhaut, 4° Pisces 04' — Royal Star, rise to fame or fall from grace, idealistic, mystical, visionary, lofty ideals kept pure succeed, but if corrupted for material ends, fail. Philosophical, attracted to occult.

Scheat, 29° Pisces 35' — Boating, swimming, lifeguards, Coast Guard, the Navy, drowning, floods, misfortune, suffering, love of language, erratic, grief, jealous, isolation, foot ailments, neuroses, creates own problems, artistry.

The Royal Stars, also called the Watchers, the Guardians, or the Four Corners of the Universe, were so-called because they were used in ancient times to reckon the locations of other objects in the heavens. Each one was found at the approximate midpoint of each of the fixed constellations in those times (Taurus, Leo, Scorpio, and Aquarius). The Royal Stars are Aldebaran (Taurus), Regulus (Leo), Antares (Scorpio), and Fomalhaut (Aquarius).

Suggested Reading and References, Level II

Note: Books under the heading of one level are not repeated on successive levels. Assume that book recommendations are cumulative. Preparation for each level assumes familiarity with material from prior levels.

Although in many instances a book was originally published at an earlier date – especially some astrology classics – only the most recent publication date and publisher are listed, to facilitate finding titles online and in bookstores as per their present-day availability.

You can find books on this list, and those in the succeeding levels, including scarce and out-of-print books, through Internet searches of one or more of the following sites:

- www.allbookstores.com
- www.astrologyetal.com
- www.amazon.com
- www.half.com
- www.barnesandnoble.com
- www.powells.com

In the case of self-published titles, an information source is specified with the entry.

General and Miscellaneous

Arroyo, Stephen. *Astrology, Karma, and Transformation: The Inner Dimensions of the Birth Chart.* CRCS Publications. 1993.

Ashman, Bernie. *Roadmap to your Future: Progressions & Transits.* ACS. 1994.

Campion, Nicholas. *The Practical Astrologer.* Harry N. Abrams. 1987.

Crane, Joseph. *A Practical Guide to Traditional Astrology.* A.R.H.A.T. 1998.

Dobyns, Zipporah. *The Node Book.* AFA. 2010.

Ebertin, Reinhold. *Applied Cosmobiology, 4th & revised edition.* AFA. 2006.

Epstein, Meira B. *Excellence in Astrology: Preparation Material for Certification Exams, Level-II; Secondary Progression Calculation; Solar Arc Calculation; Astronomy for Astrologers (Advanced); Astrology Beyond the Basics.* 2013. Available from Publisher Dr. Winai Ouypornprasert at iuf_6@yahoo.com.

Filbey, John and Peter Filbey. *The Astrologer's Companion.* Aquarian Press. 1986.

Forrest, Steven. *The Night Speaks: A Meditation on the Astrological World View: Trace the Wonder of Astrology and the Human/Cosmos Connection.* ACS. 1993.

Hand, Robert. *Horoscope Symbols.* Schiffer Publishing. 1981.

Hand, Robert. *Night and Day: Planetary Sect in Astrology.* A.R.H.A.T. 1995.

Henson, Donna. *The Vertex: The Third Angle.* AFA. 2003.

Holden, Ralph William. *The Elements of House Division.* L. N. Fowler Co., Ltd. 1977.

Jayne, Charles. *Best of Charles Jayne: (Book of His Books).* AFA. 2009.

Lamb, Terry. *Cycles of Childhood.* (Monogram). Self-published. 1996. Available at Terry@TerryLamb.net.

Lehman, J. Lee, Ph.D. *Classical Astrology for Modern Living: From Ptolemy to Psychology & Back Again.* Whitford Press. 2000.

Mann, A.T. *The Round Art of Astrology: An Illustrated Guide to Theory and Practice.* Vega Books. 2003.

March, Marion D. and Joan McEvers. *The Only Way to Learn Astrology, Vol. 3: Horoscope Analysis, 2nd edition.* ACS. 2009.

Morin, Jean Baptiste. *Astrologia Gallica.* AFA. Books 13, 14, 15, 19. 2007; Book 16, 2008; Book 17, 2008; Book 18, 2004; Book 21, 2008; Book 22, 1994; Book 23, 2002; Book 24, 2005; Book 25, 2008; Book 26, 2010.

Pottenger, Maritha. *Astrology, The Next Step.* ACS. 1998.

Pottenger, Maritha. *The East Point and the Antivertex.* ACS. 1996.

Ruperti, Alexander. *Cycles of Becoming.* Earthwalk School of Astrology Publishing. 2005.

Sakoian, Frances and Louis S. Acker. *The Astrologer's Handbook,* Reprint edition. Quill, A Harper Resource Book. 1993.

Seymour, Percy. *Astrology: The Evidence of Science,* Revised edition. Arkana. 1991.

Welsh, Lorraine and Alphee Lavoie and Mary Downing (ed.). *Essentials of Intermediate Astrology,* articles anthology on Level II material. Everson, Inc., 1995.

Westin, Leigh. *Beyond the Solstice by Declination.* Gheminee. 1999.

Lunar and Planetary Phases

George, Demetra. *Finding Our Way Through the Dark.* ACS. 1995.

Robertson, Marc. *Not a Sign in the Sky but a Living Person.* Astrology Center of the Northwest. 1975.

Rudhyar, Dane. *The Lunation Cycle: A Key to the Understanding of Personality.* Aurora Press. 1967.

Asteroids and Chiron

Clow, Barbara Hand. *Chiron: Rainbow Bridge Between Inner and Outer Planets*, 2nd edition. Llewellyn. 1999.

George, Demetra and Douglas Bloch. *Asteroid Goddesses: The Mythology, Psychology, and Astrology of the Re-Emerging Feminine.* Revised edition. Nicolas-Hays, Inc. 2003.

Pottenger, Rique, Zipporah Dobyns, Neil F. Michelsen. *The Asteroid Ephemeris 1900-2050 (Ceres, Pallas, Juno, Vesta, Chiron, and the Black Moon Lilith),* Second edition. Starcrafts Publishing. 2008.

Reinhart, Melanie. *Chiron and the Healing Journey*, 3rd revised edition. Starwalker Press. 2010.

Fixed Stars

Brady, Bernadette. *Brady's Book of Fixed Stars.* Red Wheel/Weiser. 2011.

Ebertin, Reinhold and Georg Hoffmann. *Fixed Stars and Their Interpretation.* AFA. 2009.

Robson, Vivian. *The Fixed Stars and Constellations in Astrology.* Astrology Classics. 2005.

Rosenberg, Diana K., *Secrets of the Ancient Skies, Vol. I and II*. Self-published. 2012. Available at www.ye-stars.com.

Transits, Progressions, and Directions

Blaschke, Robert. *Progressions (Astrology: A Language of Life, Vol. I)*. Earthwalk School of Astrology Publishing. 1998.

Brady, Bernadette. *Predictive Astrology: The Eagle and the Lark*. Red Wheel/Weiser. 1998.

Dobyns, Zipporah. *Progressions, Directions, and Rectification*. AFA. 2011.

Forrest, Steven. *The Changing Sky,* 2nd edition. Seven Paws Press. 2008.

Hand, Robert. *Planets in Transit: Life Cycles for Living,* Expanded edition. Whitford Press. 2002.

Hastings, Nancy. *Secondary Progressions: Time to Remember*. Red Wheel/Weiser. 1984.

Jayne, Charles. *Progressions and Directions*. AFA. 2011.

Lundsted, Betty. *Planetary Cycles: That Get You From Beginning To End Without A Guide*. Red Wheel/Weiser. 1993.

Lundsted, Betty. *Transits: The Time of Your Life,* 2nd edition. Red Wheel/Weiser. 1980.

March, Marion D. and Joan McEvers. *The Only Way to Learn About Tomorrow, Vol. 4,* 2nd edition. ACS. 2010.

Negus, Joan. *Astro-Alchemy: Making the Most of Your Transits*. ACS. 1987.

Pottenger, Maritha. *Unveiling Your Future: Progressions Made Easy.* ACS. 1998.

Robertson, Marc. *The Transit of Saturn.* AFA. 1976.

Sakoian, Frances and Louis Acker. *Transits Simplified.* AFA. 2009.

Sasportas, Howard. *The Gods of Change: Pain, Crisis and the Transits of Uranus, Neptune, and Pluto*, 2nd edition. The Wessex Astrologer. 2007.

Simms, Maria Kay. *Future Signs: How to Make Astrological Predictions.* ACS. 1996.

Sullivan, Erin. *Saturn in Transit: Boundaries of Mind, Body, and Soul*, 2nd edition. Red Wheel/Weiser. 2000.

Townley, John. *Astrological Cycles and Life Crisis Periods.* Red Wheel/Weiser. 1984.

Tyl, Noel. *Solar Arcs: Astrology's Most Successful PredictiveSystem.* Llewellyn. 2001.

Study Guide for Level III

Review: Student is responsible for all material presented in the I and II Guides. Uranian/Symmetrical Astrology, Mundane, Horary and Electional Astrology, Synastry, The History of Western Astrology, Non-Western Astrology

Uranian / Symmetrical Astrology

During the early decades of the 20th century a new form of astrology was developed in Germany that is based on symmetries of planetary positions in longitude. Alfred Witte was the primary innovator in this tradition that has influenced the field of astrology in many ways. The composite chart, graphic ephemerides, solar arc directions, midpoints and harmonics are among the contributions of this tradition to Western astrology.

The 360° Dial

A metal or plastic dial, on which all 360 degrees of the zodiac are marked or numbered, is centered and secured on a blank sheet of paper. 0° of all four cardinal signs are used as reference points and are marked with long lines and labeled. The positions of all points in the horoscope are marked on the paper with small lines and appropriately labeled. House cusps, as well as signs, degrees, and minutes of planets may be added. Once the chart is drawn, the dial is no longer held secure. It can be rotated to a wide variety of points of interest for precise measurement. For those practicing Uranian/Symmetrical Astrology, professional-level astrological software is now available.

The advantages of the 360° dial over the conventional chart are:

Both major and minor aspects in the natal chart can more easily be seen because some are indicated on the dial; and/or degrees between planets can be easily counted.

Planetary pictures are simple to see. A planetary picture is a grouping of planets in a symmetrical arrangement. It may consist of a pair of planets with a third planet in their midpoint or of two or more pairs of planets having a common midpoint that may or may not be occupied by a planet or point in the horoscope. Every planetary picture actually contains two midpoints forming an axis across the dial. Such an axis of a planetary picture may also be called an axis of symmetry.

Figure 5

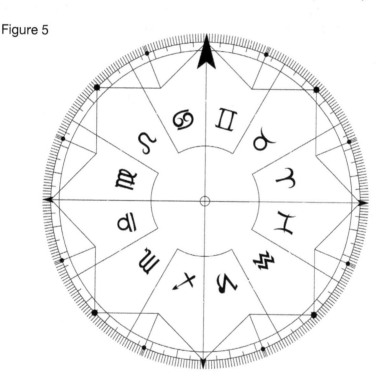

Figure 5. The 360° Dial. Zero Cancer is positioned at top and the zodiac is divided into 4 (90°), 8 (45°), 12 (30°) and 16 (22.5°) sections.. (www.alabe.com)

Planetary Pictures

A planetary picture (illustration below) is found by placing the pointer on a planet and looking for equidistant planets on either side of the pointer. As stated above, it is also possible to have the midpoint unoccupied. To determine the midpoint between two planets, place the pointer between the two planets in question so that there are the same number of degrees between each planet and the pointer. If the midpoint is occupied by a planet or point or is also the midpoint of two other planets, a planetary picture is formed.

Figure 6

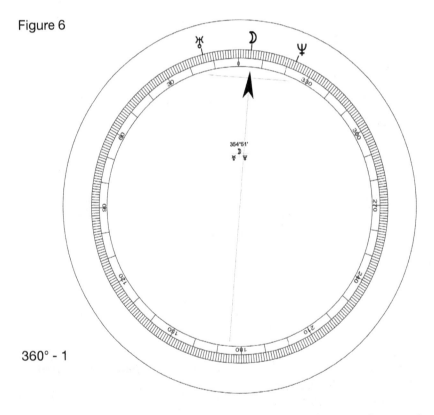

360° - 1

Figure 6 (1-4) Planetary Pictures: 360° 1: Moon at midpoint of Uranus and Neptune. 360° 2: unoccupied midpoint of Sun and Moon. 360° - 3: two midpoints (Sun/Jupiter and Saturn/Pluto) that share a common axis. 360°

Study Guide for Level III

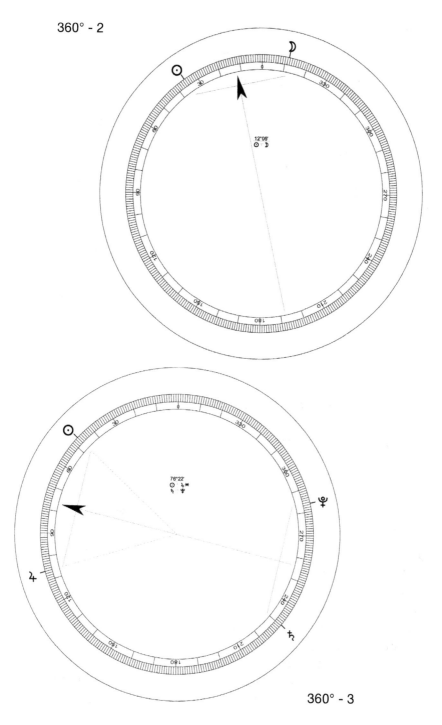

360° - 4

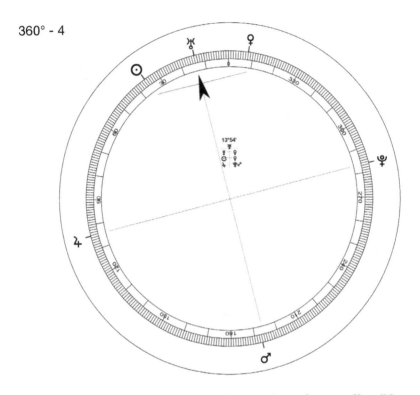

4: A direct planetary picture where two midpoints (Sun/Venus and Jupiter/Pluto) share an axis that is occupied by both Uranus and Mars. (Charts from Solar Fire software)

Hellenistic Lots and Arabic Parts as planetary pictures

Lots and Arabic Parts, techniques used in Hellenistic astrology, are sensitive degrees derived from other points in the chart. They are fundamentally groupings of points around an axis. There are various Lots or Parts covering a great deal of subjects (such as the Part of Love, Discord, Sickness, Marriage, Divorce, etc.). The typical formula for all such configurations is: A + B − C. The zodiacal degrees of the three points in this formula are used to determine a particular Lot or Part. Many modern astrologers particularly use The Part of Fortune in their work. The formula for the diurnal (day birth) Part of Fortune is Ascendant + Moon − Sun. For nocturnal births, the formula is: Ascendant + Sun − Moon.

To find the Part of Fortune for a diurnal chart, for example, the pointer of a 360° dial is placed at the midpoint of the Ascendant and the Moon (so that the same number of degrees is on either side of the pointer). Note the position of the Sun. The diurnal Part of Fortune will fall at the same degree on the opposite side of the pointer. For nocturnal births place the pointer (axis) at the midpoint of the Ascendant and Sun. Note the position of the Moon. The nocturnal Part of Fortune will fall at the same degree on the opposite side of the pointer.

It is also easy to follow transits, progressions and solar arc directions using the 360° dial. By placing the pointer of the dial on the degree of the transiting, progressed or directed body its location relative to the natal chart, including aspects and symmetry, can be seen clearly.

In calculating Lots it is expedient to convert the zodiacal degrees into absolute longitude, that is, the distance in degrees from 0 Aries.

Example: the Sun is located at 10° Aries, the Moon at 15° Gemini and the Ascendant at 20° Cancer. Ascendant (20° Cancer or 110°) + Moon (15° or 75°) − Sun (10° or 10°) = 175° or 25° Virgo. Numerous lots or parts can be generated using this basic formula.

Antiscia

Antiscia (solstice points) are the reflection points of a planet located on the opposite side of the 0° Cancer or Capricorn (solstice) axis. To calculate, note the number of degrees separating the planet from 0° Cancer or Capricorn. The point's antiscion will be at the same number of degrees on the other side of 0° Cancer or Capricorn.

The 90° Dial

To set up the dial, secure the dial over a blank piece of paper with 0° at the top. On the paper, mark a relatively long line above the 0° point and write Aries. This represents 0° of all the cardinal signs. Place the second line at the first 30° point in a counterclockwise direction and write Taurus. This represents 0° of all the fixed signs. Place the third line on the second 30° point in a counterclockwise direction and write Gemini. This represents 0° of all the mutable signs.

Figure 7

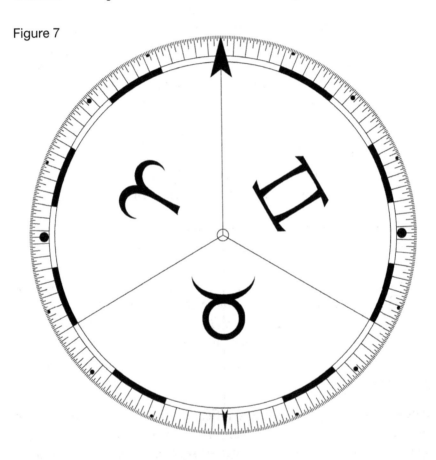

Figure 7. The 90° Dial. Four 90 degrees sections of the zodiac are superimposed on each other. The section labled Aries positions all cardinal signs, Taurus all fixed signs and Gemini all mutable signs. (www.alabe.com)

This circle consists of 90° instead of 360°. On it the points of the conventional 360° chart are reorganized in the following manner: Points in all four cardinal signs are placed in the 0° - 30° sector in the counterclockwise direction in numerical order. Continuing in a counterclockwise direction, the next 30° segment at the bottom of the chart is marked with all positions in numerical order in the fixed signs. In the final 30° segment (the upper right-hand portion of the dial) continuing in a counterclockwise direction, place all the mutable positions in numerical order.

The result is a new kind of chart on which conjunctions may represent the conjunctions found in the conventional chart but they may also represent squares and oppositions. Oppositional points on the 90° dial show both the semisquare and the sesquiquadrate.

As with the 360° dial, once the chart is drawn on the 90° dial the pointer may be rotated to any point of interest for various purposes.

Indicating Transits with the 360° and 90° dials

In order to find the aspects that a transiting planet makes to various points in a horoscope, the pointer of the dial (either 360° or 90°) is placed at the degree of the transiting planet. Scan the chart around the dial to determine which points in the horoscope are activated by any aspects that may be of interest.

Some 360° dials have marks for the conjunction, semisextile, sextile, square, trine, quincunx, opposition, as well as the semisquare and sesquiquadrate. Some dials with additional marks facilitate the discovery of less easily found aspects. These include the quintile (72°), the biquintile (144°), the septile (51°25.7'), biseptile (102°51.4'), triseptile (154°17.1'), and possibly others.

It is advisable at an early stage to form the habit of marking the dial itself in pencil or erasable pen at special points of interest (such as the above aspects), if they are not already marked on the dial.

Instead of examining a transit for a specific point in time, the dial can also be slowly rotated with the motion of a given planet for a particular period, noting aspects around the dial as they occur.

Indicating Progressions with the 360° and 90° dials

Progressions can be tracked in the same manner as above for transits.

Indicating Solar Arc Directions with the 360° and 90° dials

Determine the solar arc of the age of interest (see Level II of this study guide). Directions to and from a given planet for that age can be read by placing the pointer on the planet, noting whether any planet or point is at the number of degrees of the solar arc of interest to either side of the pointer. Mark these suggested points on the dial with a pencil or erasable pen.

As described thus far, only directions by conjunction are shown. To read other aspects, place one of the two marks for the solar arc on the planet of interest, then read off aspects around the dial as described above in transits. Then repeat the procedure with the other mark.

Only two markings are needed to designate solar arc or progressed positions using the 360° dial, these being to the right or left of the dial's pointer. In using the 90° dial for reading directions four points should be marked, two on either side of the pointer and two on either side of the 45° point on the dial.

The 360° and 90° Dials and Synastry

The planets and points of the two individuals involved in a relationship may be placed on a single sheet of paper using a dial. With different colors for each chart, place the planets and angles around the dial so that inter-aspects can be easily located.

The transits to the two charts can be tracked by placing the pointer at the position of the transiting planets and noting the aspects made to the two charts. This can be a valuable tool in timing events in the relationship.

The advantages of the 90° dial over the conventional astrogical chart are:

The 90° dial focuses on the hard aspects (conjunctions, semi squares, squares, sesquiquadrates, oppositions, and also 22°30' and 11°15' aspects).

Symmetry can be read as with the 360° dial, but with much more accuracy. In addition to the direct midpoints (conjunction and opposition point), indirect midpoints (semisquare, square, and sesquiquadrate to the conjunction and opposition point) can also be immediately seen.

Transits, progressions, and directions of hard aspects are read in the same manner as with the 360° dial. Other aspects may be read with the 90° dial, but less easily than with the 360° dial. With all aspects, however, the 90° dial is more precise.

Advantages of the 360° dial over the 90° dial:

The 360° dial can be read as a conventional chart, with intermediate house cusps indicated if desired, thus showing the house positions of the planets.

It is easy to undertake experiments with different house cusp positions and different house systems.

The direct midpoint configurations (which are the most powerful ones) are clearly shown.

Aspects of all harmonics can be read directly.

Advantages of the 90° dial over the 360° dial:

The 90° dial shows aspects and configurations of the 4th and 8th harmonics (hard aspects), indicating the most overt and obvious events, developments, and potentials.

Far more precise timing and other kinds of exactness are possible with the 90° dial.

In following solar arc directions, all the major hard aspects can be read directly without having to scan the whole wheel.

Indirect as well as direct midpoint configurations (including both midpoints and planetary pictures) can be read, although they are indistinguishable from each other.

Mundane Astrology

Knowledge of mundane astrology is required on the Level III Take Home Exam.

Mundane astrology is the branch of astrology concerned with historical and cultural trends, the study of nations, world events, meteorological conditions and earthquakes. In Classical Astrology this branch was called Universal or Natural Astrology. Each of the following is a separate field within Mundane astrology:

Political Astrology is concerned with politically organized groups such as nations or cities. It is the astrology of communities and populations of people.

Astro-geology and Astro-seismology are concerned with correlations between astrological factors and geological events such as earthquakes and volcanic eruptions. **Astro-topology** is concerned with apparent affinities between specific areas of Earth's surface and astrological factors.

Historical Astrology is concerned with patterns in history and historical trends, most often in terms of outer planet cycles.

Astrometeorology has a very long history and is concerned with weather forecasting. Until only recently it was the dominant methodology used in annual almanacs that offered weather forecasts.

Techniques employed in mundane astrology include the following:

> Natal charts of politically prominent people.
>
> Charts cast for important moments in the history of a nation, city, or community.
>
> Charts cast for eclipses and lunations.
>
> The study of major transiting phenomena.
>
> Cardinal ingress charts.

Horary Astrology

Horary is the branch of astrology that answers questions and advises the outcome of events based on a chart cast for the moment at which a question is asked, or for the moment of an event. The person asking the question is called the querent.

In contrast to humanistic natal astrology — in which the point of view is subjective, person-oriented and founded on the premise that character determines destiny — horary is objective, event-oriented and founded on the premise that events determine destiny.

Planetary rulers of house cusps are significant. Houses tell about certain circumstances and things, and aspects between planets tell about the relationships of the people or things involved.

In addition to answering simple "yes" or "no" questions, one can time future events and determine the direction or location of people, places, and things with a horary chart.

Other terms and factors of horary astrology with which the student should become familiar are:

> Besiegement
> Impedition or Refranation
> Translation of light
> Decanates
> Peregrine planets
> Considerations against judgment
> Derived houses
> Meaning of retrograde planets
> Use of dignities
> Significance of fixed stars
> Use of the Moon's Nodes, lunations, eclipses

Derived houses

House meanings can be determined from other house meanings. This is called the "house of the house" or "turning the wheel." For example, the client's sister's lover is described by the seventh house—the fifth house (lovers) from the third house (brothers and sisters) of the first house (the client.)

Inception Charts

This broadly refers to any chart that gives information based upon a given moment of time. One could say that a natal chart is inceptional, as a person's life is read from the moment of birth; nonetheless, an event chart assesses the exact moment of the event for its meaning and outcome. Commonly they are used for large-scale occurrences, such as earthquakes or political events, or on more personal levels, like an award or layoff notice.

A decumbiture chart is one type of event chart. It is cast for a person taking to his or her sick bed and will show the timing of changes in the condition of the person and the outcome of the sickness.

Electional Astrology

Electional astrology is required on the Level III Take-Home Exam.

Electional astrology is concerned with selecting the most favorable moment for initiating an undertaking. Electional charts can be created for such projects as the opening of a business, the timing of a wedding or partnership, and the start of a journey, among other types of events.. There are basically three approaches to electing a time.

Radical Elections. Selecting a chart for a specific future event that will be related to the natal chart of the person (or persons) involved in the project. Natal configurations, progressions, and transits to the natal chart are used to determine a favorable time.

Mundane Elections. Using charts of eclipses, major conjunctions, and ingresses as reference points for an election. This approach is mostly considered for elections involving large groups of people.

Ephemeral Elections. Using only the actual transiting positions and the relationship of the planets as references. If one erects a chart, the degrees on the angles become significant.

Synastry (Astrology of Relationships)

This area involves the investigation of natal charts, with emphasis on relationship potential. There are several areas of focus:

Comparison — Zodiacal compatibility with signs, elements, and modes of personal planets.

Inter-aspects — The aspects between the charts, including important midpoints.

Similarities/Differences — The planetary dynamics between the charts.

The Composite Chart
(Calculation of a Composite Chart is required for the Level III exam)

A composite chart is a midpoint chart of two or more natal charts. Erecting this chart describes a couple or group as a single entity. There are two methods of erecting a composite chart:

Find the midpoint of the two Midheavens. Look up the composite Midheaven in a Tables of Houses and calculate the houses for the latitude of the relationship.

Calculate the midpoints of all the house cusps. Erect a chart using the midpoints of each house cusp.

For either method, **calculate the midpoint of each pair of planets.** (both Suns, Moons, etc.).

Transits to the planets and points in the composite chart can be used to describe developments in the relationship.

A progressed composite chart can be created by progressing each of the natal charts to a given date and calculating the midpoints of the house cusps and planets of the two charts by one of the two methods for erecting a composite chart.

Relationship Chart

A relationship chart (sometimes referred to as a Davison chart) is calculated for the actual midpoint in time and space of two natal charts. One must take into account such factors as leap years, etc. When the date, time, longitude and latitude is determined, a chart is erected using this new data. This chart can be used with transits, progressions, and solar arc directions, as one would with a natal chart.

Solar and Lunar Returns

Solar or lunar returns are transit charts calculated for the day of the return of the Sun or Moon to its exact natal position. A solar return symbolizes the annual recharging and rechanneling of conscious energy. A lunar return symbolizes the monthly recharging and rechanneling of emotional energy.

The prominence of certain houses and planets in a return chart indicates possible external manifestations of energy in a particular arena of life. The natal houses so affected also suggest the ultimate meaning that the experiences of the year or month will have on the life as a whole.

Solar and lunar returns are most meaningful when interpreted in light of the natal chart. Their value is extremely limited if restricted to an attempt to predict specific events. They are used most advantageously as a guide toward the most productive direction one can take within a specific time-span.

Solar or lunar return charts may be calculated for the birthplace, the place of residence, or one's location at the time of the return.

The History of Astrology in the West and NonWestern Astrology

A short summary of the history of astrology is found in Appendix III and references for publications on this subject are found in the following bibliography. All those who practice astrology should be familiar with its history. Knowledge of the past allows us to put the present in perspective and keeps us from making the same mistakes again. History also preserves developments and discoveries that can be recovered for use or improvement in the present. The astrological traditions that developed in India, China and Mesoamerica are also discussed in Appendix III.

Suggested Reading and References, Level III

Note: Books under the heading of one level are not repeated on successive levels. Assume that book recommendations are cumulative. Preparation for each level assumes familiarity with material from prior levels.

Although in many instances a book was originally published at an earlier date – especially some astrology classics – only the most recent publication date and publisher are listed, to facilitate finding titles online and in bookstores as per their present-day availability.

You can find books on this list, and those in the succeeding level, including scarce and out-of-print books, through Internet searches of one or more of the following sites:

- www.allbookstores.com
- www.astrologyetal.com
- www.amazon.com
- www.half.com
- www.barnesandnoble.com
- www.powells.com

In the case of self-published titles, an information source is specified with the entry.

Dials and Symmetry

Ebertin, Reinhold. *The Combination of Stellar Influences.* AFA. 2004.

Kimmel, Eleanora. *Cosmobiology for the 21st Century.* AFA. 2000.

Harding, Michael and Charles Harvey. *Working with Astrology: The Psychology of Harmonics, Midpoints, and Astrocartography, Revised edition.* Consider Publications. 1998.

Munkasey, Michael. *Midpoints: Unleashing the Power of the Planets.* ACS. 1991.

Rudolph, Ludwig & Hermann Lefeldt. *Alfred Witte's Rules for Planetary-Pictures: The Astrology of Tomorrow.* Penelope Publications. 1999.

Simms, Maria Kay. *Dial Detective: Investigation with the 90° Dial, Revised second edition.* Starcrafts Publishing. 2001.

Mundane Astrology

Baigent, Michael, Nicholas Campion and Charles Harvey. *Mundane Astrology: An Introduction to the Astrology of Nations and Groups, 2nd edition.* Thorsons Publishing. 1995.

Campion, Nicholas. *The Book of World Horoscopes.* The Wessex Astrologer. 2004.

Carter, C.E.O, "An Introduction to Political Astrology"; Green, H.S., "Mundane or National Astrology"; and "Raphael's Mundane Astrology". *Mundane Astrology: The Astrology of Nations and States.* Astrology Classics. 2005.

Dodson, Carolyn. *Horoscopes of the U.S. States and Cities.* AFA. 1975.

Johndro, L. Edward. *The Earth in the Heavens: Ruling Degrees of Cities, How to Find and Use Them.* Sun Publishing. 1991.

McEvers, Joan, ed. *The Astrology of the Macrocosm: New Directions in Mundane Astrology.* Llewellyn. 1990.

Moore, Moon. *The Book of World Horoscopes: The Astrological Gazeteer of the Modern Geo-Political World.* Seek-It Publications. 1980.

Penfield, Marc H. *Horoscopes of the USA and Canada*. AFA. 2005.

Tarnas, Richard. *Cosmos and Psyche: Intimations of a New World View*. Plume/Penguin. 2007.

Tyl, Noel. *Prediction in Astrology: A Master Volume of Technique and Practice*. Llewellyn. 1995.

Horary and Electional Astrology

Barclay, Olivia. *Horary Astrology Rediscovered: A Study in Classical Astrology*. Whitford Press. 1990.

Cornelius, Geoffrey. Moment of Astrology: Origins in Divination. The Wessex Astrologer. 2005.

Frawley, John. *The Horary Textbook – Revised edition*. Apprentice Books. 2014.

Goldstein-Jacobson, Ivy M. *Simplified Horary Astrology: Reprint edition*. Ivy M. Goldstein-Jacobson/Frank Severy Publishing. 1975.

Hamaker-Zondag, Karen. *Handbook of Horary Astrology*. Red Wheel/Weiser. 1993.

Jones, Marc Edmund. *Horary Astrology: Practical Techniques for Problem Solving*. Aurora Press. 1993.

Lavoie, Alphee. *Lose This Book. and Find It With Horary*, 2nd edition. Air Software. 2008.

Lehman, J. Lee, Ph.D. *The Martial Art of Horary Astrology*. Whitford Press. 2002.

Lilly, William. *Christian Astrology (three volumes in one)*. Cosimo Classics. 2011.

Louis, Anthony. *Horary Astrology: Plain & Simple: Fast & Accurate Answers to Real World Questions.* Llewellyn. 2002.

March, Marion D. and Joan McEvers. *The Only Way to Learn About Horary and Electional Astrology, Volume 6, 2nd edition.* ACS. 1994.

Scofield, Bruce. *The Timing of Events: Electional Astrology.* Astrolabe. 1986.

Watters, Barbara H. *Horary Astrology and the Judgment of Events.* AFA. 2012..

Zain, C.C. *Horary Astrology: How to Erect and Judge a Horoscope, Course VIII.* Church of Light. 1976.

Synastry

Arroyo, Stephen. *Relationships and Life Cycles: Astrological Patterns of Personal Experience.* CRCS Publications. 1993.

Ashman, Bernie. *SignMates: An Astrological Guide to Love and Intimacy.* Llewellyn. 2000.

Ebertin, Reinhold. *The Cosmic Marriage.* AFA. 2004.

Forrest, Jodie and Steven Forrest. *Skymates: Love, Sex and Evolutionary Astrology, Vol. I., Revised expanded edition.* Seven Paws Press. 2002.

Forrest, Steven & Jodie Forrest. *Skymates: The Composite Chart, Vol. II.* Seven Paws Press. 2005.

Hand, Robert. *Planets in Composite: Analyzing Human Relationships.* Schiffer Publishing. 1975.

Lamb, Terry. *Born to Be Together: Astrology, Relationships, and the Soul.* Hay House. 1998.

March, Marion D. and Joan McEvers, *The Only Way to Learn About Relationships: Synastry Techniques, Volume 5*, 2nd edition. ACS. 2009.

Negus, Joan. *Interpreting Composite and Relationship Charts*. ACS. 1996.

Neville, E.W. *Planets in Synastry: Astrologic Patterns of Relationship*. Schiffer Publishing. 1997.

Pottenger, Maritha. *Your Starway to Love: Better Romance With Astrology*, 2nd edition. ACS. 1996.

Sargent, Lois Haines. *How to Handle Your Human Relations*. AFA. 1995..

Townley, John. *Composite Charts: The Astrology of Relationships*. Llewellyn. 2000.

Townley, John. *Planets in Love: Exploring Your Emotional and Sexual Needs*. Schiffer Publishing. 1997.

Solar and Lunar Returns

Louis, Anthony. *The Art of Forecasting using Solar Returns*. The Wessex Astrologer. 2008.

Merriman, Raymond A. *The New Solar Return Book of Prediction*, Revised edition. Seek-It Publications. 1998.

Shea, Mary. *Planets in Solar Returns: A Yearly Guide for Transformation & Growth*, Revised edition. Twin Stars. 1998.

Volguine, Alexandre. *The Technique of Solar Returns*, 3rd edition. ASI Publishers. 1976.

History of Astrology in the West

General

Bobbrick, Benson. *The Fated Sky: Astrology in History*. Simon & Schuster. 2006.

Campion, Nicholas. *The Great Year: Astrology, Millenarianism, and History in the Western Tradition*. Penguin Arkana. 1995.

Campion, Nicholas. *A History of Western Astrology, Volume I: The Ancient and Classical Worlds*. Bloomsbury Academic Press. 2009.

Campion, Nicholas. *A History of Western Astrology, Volume II: The Medieval and Modern Worlds*. Bloomsbury Academic Press. 2009.

Holden, James Herschel. *A History of Horoscopic Astrology: From the Babylonian Period to the Modern Age*, 3rd edition. AFA. 2013.

Kitson, Annabella, ed. *History and Astrology: Clio and Urania Confer*. Mnemosyne Press. 1995.

Naylor, Phyllis Irene Hannah. *Astrology: An Historical Examination*. Maxwell. 1967.

Smoller, Laura Ackerman. *History, Prophecy, and the Stars*. Princeton University Press. 1994.

Whitfield, Peter. *Astrology: A History*. Harry N. Abrams. 2001.

Mesopotamia and Egypt

Baigent, Michel. *From the Omens of Babylon: Astrology and Ancient Mesopotamia*. Penguin Arkana. 1994.

Lindsay, Jack. *Origins of Astrology*. Barnes & Noble Books. 1971.

Reiner, Erica and David Edwin Pingree. *Babylonian Planetary Omens: Enuma anu Enlil, Tablet 63, The Venus Tablet of Ammisaduqua*. Undena Publications. 1975.

Greece and Rome

Barton, Tamsyn. *Ancient Astrology*. Routledge. 1994.

Cramer, Frederick H. *Astrology in Roman Law and Politics (Memoirs of the American Philosophical Society, V. 37)*. Literary Licensing. 2011.

Neugebauer, O. and H. B. Van Hoesen. *Greek Horoscopes (Memoirs of the American Philosophical Society)*. American Philosophical Society. 1987.

Ptolemy, Claudius. *Ptolemy's Tetrabiblos, Or Quadripartite: Being Four Books of the Influence of the Stars*. Ulan Press. 2012.

Tester, Jim. *A History of Western Astrology*. BOYE6. 1990.

Middle Ages

Thorndike, Lynn. *History of Magic and Experimental Science, 8 volumes*. Columbia University Press. 1958.

Wedel, Theodore Otto. *The Medieval Attitude Toward Astrology, Particularly in England*. Kessinger Publishing. 2010.

The Renaissance and the Scientific Revolution

Allen, Don Cameron. *The Star-Crossed Renaissance: The Quarrel About Astrology and its Influence in England*. Literary Licensing. 2011.

Butterfield, Herbert. *The Origins of Modern Science, Revised edition*. The Free Press. 1997.

Caspar, Max. *Kepler.* Dover Publications. 1993.

Curry, Patrick. *Prophecy and Power: Astrology in Early Modern England.* Princeton University Press. 1989.

French, Peter J. *John Dee: The World of an Elizabethan Magus.* Hippocrene Books. 1989.

Grafton, Anthony. *Cardano's Cosmos: The Worlds and Works of a Renaissance Astrologer.* Harvard University Press. 2001.

Koestler, Arthur. *The Watershed: A Biography of Johannes Kepler.* Doubleday. 1960.

Parker, Derek. *Familiar to All: William Lilly and Astrology in the Seventeenth Century.* Jonathan Cape. 1975.

Thomas, Keith. *Religion and the Decline of Magic.* Penguin. 2012.

Yates, Frances A. *Giordano Bruno and the Hermetic Tradition.* University of Chicago Press. 1991.

The Twentieth Century

Howe, Ellic. *Astrology and Psychological Warfare During World War II, Revised and condensed edition.* Rider. 1972.

Astrology of India, China and Mesoamerica

India

Braha, James T. *Ancient Hindu Astrology for the Modern Western Astrologer.* Hermetician Press. 1993.

Dreyer, Ronnie Gale. Vedic *Astrology: A Guide to the Fundamentals of Jyotish*. Weiser Books. 1997.

Frawley, David. *Astrology of the Seers: A Guide to Vedic/Hindu Astrology*, 5th edition. Motilal Banarsidass Publishers. 2013.

Harness, Dennis, Ph.D. *The Nakshatras: The Lunar Mansions of Vedic Astrology*. Lotus Press. 1999.

Hathaway, Edith. *In Search of Destiny: Biography, History & Culture As Told Through Vedic Astrology*. Vintage Vedic Press. 2012.

Roebuck, Valerie J. *The Circle of Stars: An Introduction to Indian Astrology*. Element Books. 1992.

China

De Kermadec, Jean-Michel Huon. *The Way to Chinese Astrology: The Four Pillars of Destiny*. HarperCollins. 1983.

Walters, Derek. *Chinese Astrology: Interpreting the Revelations of the Celestial Messengers*. Thorsons Publishing. 1993.

Mesoamerica

Aveni, Anthony F. *Skywatchers: A Revised and Updated Version of Skywatchers of Ancient Mexico*. University of Texas Press. 2001.

Scofield, Bruce. *Day-Signs: Native American Astrology From Ancient Mexico*. One Reed Publications. 1997.

Scofield, Bruce. *Signs of Time: An Introduction to Mesoamerican Astrology*. One Reed Publications. 1997.

Study Guide for Level IV

Testing is based on exams or exercises prepared and then submitted. All applicants are required to submit a rectification and must choose a track (technical research, general research, consulting, or instructional) for the remainder of Level IV requirements.

Note: All applications for rectification and testing within the chosen Level IV track should be accompanied by the required fee. See www.astrologersalliance.org or contact the NCGR-PAA Education Director at education@astrologersalliance.org for fee information and specific administrative procedures.

Rectification

All candidates for Level IV certification must rectify a chart before starting their chosen track. The candidate should select a chart of an individual whose birth time is unknown.

Upon completion of the rectification, all the materials pertaining to it should be sent to the NCGR-PAA Education Director. A self-assigned code number should appear on the written rectification materials. The candidate's name should not appear on any test materials submitted, but should be listed on a separate sheet of paper only.
The defense should consist of the following, the written parts of which are to be typed and double-spaced:

1. a one page copy of the biography, including six to ten events with dates.

2. a two page explanation of your rectification procedure, listing the techniques that you used. This must include at least three different timing techniques such as transits, secondary progressions, solar arc directions, eclipses, etc. Be sure to indicate all the main steps in the process from beginning to end.

3. a three to fifteen page defense of how you arrived at your result. At

least two of the techniques chosen should be applied to each of the six events. They need not be the same ones for all events.

4. a one to three page description of how your chart fits the biographical sketch.

5. a rectified chart with date, time, and place of birth.

Each statement of evidence for the accuracy of the rectified chart must include the following information: AspectING body/point, zodiacal position; aspectED (natal, progressed, relocated, etc.) body/point, zodiacal position; orb; declination.

- For example: Divorce, September 19, 1965

- Transiting Uranus (15° Virgo 22') square natal Ascendant (15° Gemini 28'), orb of 6 minutes

- Uranus (often referred to as "the planet of divorce") symbolizes radical or drastic change often in the form of a reversal aspecting the Ascendant (which is the partnership axis).

    Copies of all charts (or listings) necessary to accomplish and judge the rectification must be included. For example, progressed charts (or listings) in support of progressed positions cited, listing of all solar arcs when applicable, relocation charts, charts of significant other persons where synastry is used.

    Once the rectification is passed the candidate has the option of taking any (or all) certifications. One is for consulting, another for technical research, another for general research, and the fourth for instructor in astrology. Upon passing all requirements the candidate will receive a document suitable for framing which will appropriately recognize and certify the candidate's achievement.

    The successful candidate also will have the distinction of placing the letters C.A., NCGR-PAA after his or her name, signifyiing Certified Astrologer, NCGR-PAA. The candidate's name will also be added to the NCGR-PAA Certified Astrologers listing on its web site: www.astrologersalliance.org.

Examination for Professional Research Astrologer: Scientific, Technical, Statistical Option

General description: exploration of areas of astrology utilizing generally accepted scientific (physical or social) and/or statistical methods.

First, a proposal must be submitted to the NCGR-PAA Education Director along with the required fee. The proposal should include:

- Proposed topic (50 to 100 words)
- Proposed hypotheses (50 to 100 words)
- Proposed methodology (50 to 100 words)

You will be notified of acceptance, conditional acceptance, or rejection. You can proceed to research the topic as agreed upon.

The final result should be a research paper of no less than 15 pages, nor more than 40 typewritten and double-spaced pages in length, although exceptions may be granted. In this paper you are expected to state hypotheses and methodology clearly, as well as meaningful results, be they negative or positive.

For the conventions of manuscript preparation, footnotes, bibliography, etc., it may be helpful to refer to the MLA Style Manual, Third Edition 2008, Modern Language Association, available through www.mla.org.

The research paper should be submitted in duplicate to the NCGR-PAA Education Director. It will then be evaluated for acceptance or rejection by two examiners who must agree on the final result.

Examination for Professional Research Astrologer: General Studies Option

General description: exploration of less rigorously defined areas of astrology such as case studies or interpretive approaches and symbolism. In many cases methods and materials may be drawn from those academic disciplines known as the humanities—such as psychology, history, philosophy, literature, the arts, philology, mythology.

First, submit a proposal to the NCGR-PAA Education Director along with the required fee. The proposal should include:

- Proposed topic and reasons for choice (50 to 100 words)
- Proposed line of investigation (50 to 100 words)
- List 5-15 essential texts and references for your topic, if applicable

You will be notified of acceptance, conditional acceptance, or rejection. You can proceed to research the topic as agreed upon.

Guidelines for the General Research Track

1. Hypotheses

What questions are being asked in the project?

What is already known about the topic? (Review of principle literature on the subject.) State the practical or philosophical value of the study.

2. Project design

State the sources of information that will be consulted to support this study.

Describe guidelines and procedure you plan to follow.

3. Results

Conclusions should be relevant to the original objective of the study.

Describe the contribution this study makes to the knowledge of the field.

If your conclusions contradict generally accepted assumptions, defend your position.

The final result should be a research paper of no less than 15 pages, nor more than 35 typewritten and double-spaced pages in length, although exceptions may be granted. In this paper you are expected to state hypotheses and methodology clearly, as well as meaningful results, be they negative or positive.

For the conventions of manuscript preparation, footnotes, bibliography, etc., it may be helpful to refer to the MLA Style Manual, Third Edition 2008, Modern Language Association, available through www.mla.org.

The above research paper should be submitted in duplicate to the NCGR-PAA Education Director. It will then be evaluated for acceptance or rejection by two examiners who must agree on the final result.

Examination for the Professional Consulting Astrologer

Application and Procedure

To apply for this examination, send a resume to the NCGRPAA Education Director, stating your counseling knowledge/experience. Enclose the required fee along with your letter and application.

When you apply, please have two written character references sent separately to the NCGRPAA Education Director. Both letters should be from individuals who know you in an area of life unrelated to astrology. References from relatives cannot be accepted.

After receipt of your application and examination fee, you will then select your own client, who should not be a relative or close friend. You will then proceed as you would with any professional relationship.

As part of the examination, you are required to record and submit a 90-minute cassette or compact disc (CD), in duplicate, of the session. The client should be informed of this procedure and its purpose as an evaluation tool for your candidacy as a professional consulting astrologer. You may wish to suggest to the client that he or she has the option of recording the session as well; the client should then bring along a separate recording device for this purpose.

The Examination

There are three sections to the examination:

1. Preparation for the consulting session.

2. The consulting session. (Natal plus projection for at least 6 months.)

3. Your critique of the session.

Sections 1 and 3 are to be presented as written commentaries;

Section 2 is to be presented as a 90-minute cassette or compact disc (CD).

DO NOT IDENTIFY YOURSELF on any materials except by a self-assigned code number. Neither should your name be on the recording submitted, unless spoken inadvertently by the client. List your name separately on a sheet of paper submitted with your materials.

In any case, do not edit, change, delete, or erase any segment of the recorded session.

Furthermore, every effort should be made to protect the client's identity. Therefore, on the materials you submit, the client's name should not be revealed. Only you, the client, and possibly the NCGR-PAA Education Director will know the client's identity. (A first name alone is unlikely to reveal the client's identity on the recording.)

Preparation for the Consulting Session

After you have studied the chart but before you see the client, please prepare:

1. Copies of the charts and any other technical materials you normally use.

2. A written analysis of your understanding and expectations of the client; and how you would handle any sensitive issues that could arise based on these expectations. Be sure to justify your remarks with the astrological indications which lead to your judgments. (Maximum of 10 pages, no less than 5 pages, typed and double-spaced.)

3. A written essay as follows: Relying on your own personal value system, describe what you consider to be your professional and ethical standards as a consulting astrologer, addressing the topics listed below. Please respond to each topic with a paragraph or two. The purpose of this essay is to help you define and clarify your thinking about professional and ethical issues. There are not necessarily any right or wrong answers. You will be evaluated only on how well you defend your positions.

    a. Client confidentiality

    b. Privacy and appropriateness of session location and setting

    c. Maintaining time structure of session

    d. Establishing fees

e. Setting a cancellation/lateness policy

f. Allowing another person (or persons) to be present at the session.

g. Predicting death or serious illness of client/or a client's loved one

h. The suitability and use of astrological jargon

i. Friendships with clients outside the session

j. Emotional involvement with client within the session

Two typed copies of both the written analysis and the written essay, along with pertinent charts and other materials you use, must be mailed to the NCGR-PAA Education Director and postmarked before you meet the client.

Consulting Session

Record the consulting session on cassette or compact disc (CD). (Please use one 90-minute cassette or CD even though the session may run shorter.)

Post-Consultation Critique

Following the session, please prepare a written evaluation of the client, the events of the session, and your own performance. This should be based both on the chart and your experience of the session. This is also an opportunity to comment on matters you chose not to cover during the recording of the session. The critique should be no less than five and no longer than ten typed, double-spaced pages.

Two copies of the recording and two copies of the post-consultation critique and any other paperwork must be mailed to the NCGR-PAA Education Director and postmarked within a week after the consultation.

Examiners and Criteria for Judgment

The NCGR-PAA Education Director will submit your written materials and recording simultaneously to two examiners who do not live in your geographical location. If they both agree, their decision stands. However, if one passes the candidate and one fails, the recording and papers go to a third examiner, whose judgment will be the tie-breaker.

Your identity will not be revealed to the examiners. Their identities will not be revealed to you.

Your skill and wisdom in consulting, your ability to synthesize, your flexibility in meeting the reality of the client, and your technical expertise will be the examiners' criteria for judgment.

Consultations are not to be a mere recitation of educational/astrological information about everything in the client's chart. You are not teaching a class; you are conducting a consultation in which the client's needs are paramount. Wisdom in consulting requires skill beyond knowledge of astrological technique. The criteria of judgment for the examiners evaluating your tape will include your ability to listen effectively as well as speak, to synthesize information, and to be flexible in meeting the reality of your client in an ethical and responsible manner.

The NCGR-PAA Education Director will inform you of the examiners' decision.

Examination for Professional Instructor in Astrology

After contacting the NCGR-PAA Education Director and submitting the appropriate fee and application, the candidate is to provide:

1. A curriculum for one course in astrology, including:

    a. Scope (what will be covered in the course) and sequence (how it fits in with the broader educational programs of learning astrology).

b. Syllabus

c. Booklist

d. Reading, homework assignments, and lesson plans for each lesson in the course.

e. List of materials to be used in class (handouts, etc.).

f. Statement of how students will be evaluated.

g. Statement regarding the business side — how the instructor will cultivate students, what pricing will be used, and how the instructor will be compensated, where classes will be held, and what kind of structure will be established for students (contracts, application forms, etc.).

2. In-depth materials for one class, including:

   a. A recording (cassette or compact disc (CD)) of the candidate's verbal presentation, 90-120 minutes in length. (Another form of proof may be possible, but a proposal for such must be submitted to the NCGR-PAA Education Director for approval).

   b. A detailed outline/plan for the class.

   c. Copies of handouts or overhead transparencies to be used in class. (Masters for transparencies rather than actual transparencies are acceptable.).

   d. Any homework or reading assignments.

   e. A brief explanation of how everything associated with the class relates to:

      i. its scope and purpose

ii. its role in the sequence of the course of which it is a part

f. If it is a separate unit itself (such as a stand-alone workshop), explain what benefit it provides the student.

g. A critique of the presentation after the class is taught (3-5 pages typewritten and double-spaced) in terms of its:

   i. Organization
   ii. Effectiveness in teaching the student
   iii. How well the ancillary materials worked to support the intended purpose of the class
   iv. How the class might be improved

All written materials, as well as the recording, should be submitted in duplicate to the NCGR-PAA Education Director, along with the application and fee.

Examiners and Criteria for Judgment

The NCGR-PAA Education Director will submit your written materials and recording simultaneously to two examiners who do not live in your geographical location. Your identity will not be revealed to them. Their identities will not be revealed to you.

In the event of conflicting judgments, your examination will be submitted to a third examiner, whose judgment will be the tiebreaker.

Your skill and wisdom in preparation, your ability to present the material to the class, your flexibility in meeting the reality of the classroom environment and feedback from students, and your technical expertise will be the examiners' criteria for judgment.

Suggested Reading and References, Level IV

Note: Books under the heading of one level are not repeated on successive levels. Assume that book recommendations are cumulative. Preparation for each level assumes familiarity with material from prior levels.

Although in many instances a book was originally published at an earlier date – especially some astrology classics – only the most recent publication date and publisher are listed, to facilitate finding titles online and in bookstores as per their present-day availability.

You can find books on this list, and those in the preceding levels, including scarce and out-of-print books, through Internet searches of one or more of the following sites:

- www.allbookstores.com
- www.astrologyetal.com
- www.amazon.com
- www.half.com
- www.barnesandnoble.com
- www.powells.com

In the case of self-published titles, an information source is specified with the entry.

Rectification

Ely, Lawrence, "Toward a General Theory of Rectification." in *Astrology's Special Measurements*, ed. Noel Tyl. Llewellyn. 1994.

Niemann, Henry. *Rectification: Known and Unknown Birthtimes.* AFA. 2013.

Tebbs, Carol A. *The Complete Book of Chart Rectification*. Llewellyn. 2008.

Tyl, Noel. *Astrology of the Famed: Startling Insights Into Their Lives*. Llewellyn. 1996.

Tyl, Noel. *Astrology Looks at History*. Llewellyn. 1995.

Research Tracks

Dean, Geoffrey, Ph.D and Arthur Mather. *Recent Advances in Natal Astrology: A Critical Review 1900-1976.*. Analogic. 1977.

Foreman, Patricia. *Computers and Astrology: A Universal User's Guide and Reference*. Good Earth Publications. 1992.

Gauquelin, Françoise. *Psychology of the Planets*. ACS. 1987.

Gauquelin, Michel. *Planetary Heredity*. ACS. 1988.

Perry, Glenn, Ph.D. *Stealing Fire from the Gods: New Directions in Astrological Research*. Self-published. 2006. Available at www.aaperry.com.

Pottenger, Mark, ed. *Astrological Research Methods, Volume I: An ISAR Anthology*. Seek-It Publications. 1995.

Sidman, Murray. *Tactics of Scientific Research: Evaluating Experimental Data in Psychology*. Cambridge Center for Behavioral Psychology. 1988.

Consulting Track

Bell, Lynn. *Planetary Threads: The Living History of FamilyDynamics in our Patterns of Relating*. Ibis Press. 2013.

Clark, Brian J. *The Sibling Constellation*. Penguin. 1999.

Cunningham, Donna. *The Consulting Astrologer's Guidebook*. Weiser Books. 1994.

Duncan, Adrian Ross. *Astrology: Transformation and Empowerment*. Red Wheel/Weiser. 2002.

Gibson, Mitchell E., M.D. *Signs of Mental Illness: An Astrological and Psychiatric Breakthrough*. Llewellyn. 1995.

Greene, Liz and Howard Sasportas. *The Development of the Personality: Seminars in Psychological Astrology, Vol. 1*. Red Wheel/Weiser. 1987.

Greene, Liz and Howard Sasportas. *Dynamics of the Unconscious: Seminars in Psychological Astrology, Vol. 2*. Weiser Books. 1988.

Greene, Liz and Howard Sasportas. *The Luminaries: The Psychology of the Sun and Moon in the Horoscope*. Red Wheel/Weiser. 1992.

Greene, Liz and Howard Sasportas. *The Inner Planets: Building Blocks of Personal Reality*. Weiser Books. 1993.

Guggenbuhl-Craig, Adolf. *Power in the Helping Professions*. Spring Publications. 1998.

Hamaker-Zondag, Karen. *Psychological Astrology*. Red Wheel/Weiser. 1990.

Hebel, Doris. *Celestial Psychology: An Astrological Guide to Growth and Transformation*. Aurora Press. 1985.

Idemon, Richard. *Through the Looking Glass*. The Wessex Astrologer. 2010.

Kennedy, Eugene and Sara C. Charles, M.D. *On Becoming a Counselor: A Basic Guide for Nonprofessional Counselors and Other Helpers*, 3rd expanded revised edition. The Crossroad Publishing Co. 2001.

Langs, Robert. *A Clinical Workbook for Psychotherapists*. Karnac Books. 1992.

Lerner, Harriet, Ph.D. *The Dance of Anger: A Woman's Guide to Changing the Patterns of Intimate Relationships*. William Morrow. 2014.

Lewis, Byron and Frank Pucelik. *Magic of NLP Demystified, Second edition*. Crown House Publishing. 2012.

Mann, A. T. *Astrology and the Art of Healing*, Paraview Press. 2004.

Mann, A. T., ed. *The Future of Astrology: Selected Essays by Modern Astrologers*. Paraview Presss. 2004.

McEvers, Joan, ed. *Astrological Counseling: The Path to Self-Actualization*. Llewellyn. 1990.

Perry, Glenn, Ph.D. *Mapping the Landscape of the Soul: Inside Psychological Astrology*. Self-published. 2013. Available at www.aaperry.com.

Perry, Glenn, Ph.D, ed. *Issues and Ethics in the Profession of Astrology*. Self-published. 2005. Available at www.aaperry.com.

Pottenger, Maritha. *Healing with the Horoscope: A Guide to Counseling*. ACS. 1991.

Reid, Linda. *Crossing the Threshold: The Astrology of Dreaming*. Penguin. 1998.

Rose, Christina. *Astrological Counselling: A Basic Guide to Astrological Themes in Person to Person Understanding*, 2nd edition. Sterling Publishing. 1983.

Sharman-Burke, Juliet and Liz Greene. *The Astrologer, the Counsellor and the Priest: Two Seminars on Astrological Counselling.* CPA Press. 2005.

Tyl, Noel. *Synthesis and Counseling in Astrology: The Professional Manual.* Llewellyn. 2002.

The subject of Ethics for Astrologers is introduced at Level I and incorporated into testing for all levels. Following here is a list of recommended articles on ethics. The entire NCGR-PAA Code of Ethics is found in Appendix I of this Study Guide.

Ethics: Recommended Articles

Arner, David. "ArtPart Forum: Ethics and Confidentiality," *The Mountain Astrologer*, October 1996.

Arner, David. "Ethics in Shades of Grey." *The Mountain Astrologer*, October/November 2001.

Arner, David. "Solving Ethical Problems," *The Astrologers Newsletter*, Boston Chapter NCGR, November 1998.

Arner, David. "Coming to Be...An NCGR Code of Ethics," *NCGR Memberletter*, February/ March 1998.

Arner, David. "Ethics Then and Now," *NCGR Memberletter*, November/December 1996.

Betts, Cynthia. "Ethics for the Practice of Astrological Consultation," *NCGR Memberletter*, August/September 1995.

Callahan, Joan C., ed. *Ethical Issues in Professional Life.* Oxford University Press. 1988. This book contains an especially recommended article, "The Ideological Use of Professional Codes" by John Kultgen. The Appendix includes ethics codes for eight professional organizations.

Crosby, Beverly. "Wednesday Morning: Reader Response," *NCGR Memberletter,* September 1992.

Cunningham, Donna. "Your Reactions to Clients," *The Mountain Astrologer,* July 1992.

Cunningham, Donna. "First Contact with the Client," *The Mountain Astrologer,* March 1992.

Finger, Lynn. "Astrology and Professionalization: Identifying the Issues," *The Mountain Astrologer,* April/May 1994.

Frigola, Francoise. "Counseling Astrology," *Aspects,* Fall 1990.

Joyce, Linda. "Ethics and Astrology: A Conflict of Interest?" *NCGR Memberletter,* June 1992.

Joyce, Linda. "Setting Boundaries: A Questionnaire," *NCGR Memberletter,* June/July 1992.

Koval, Barbara. "Philosophy and Practice," *The Mountain Astrologer,* August 1993.

Lamb, Terry. "Unconscious Communication and the Astrological Consultation," *NCGR Journal, Winter 2000/2001.*

McCabe, Eileen. "Peer Supervision in Astrology," *NCGR Memberletter,* February 1992.

Merriman, Raymond A. "Forecasting Current Events in a Professional Manner," *The Career Astrologer (PROSIG),* January 1995.

Munkasey, Michael. "Towards a Definition of Astrology," *NCGR Memberletter*, February/March 1997.

Oja, Dorothy. "Ethics, Responsibility, and Astrological Conscience," *The Mountain Astrologer*, April/May 1993.

Oja, Dorothy. "More on Ethics and Conscience in Astrology," *The Mountain Astrologer*, November 1994.

Perry, Glenn, Ph.D. "Psychological versus Predictive Astrology," *The Mountain Astrologer*, February/March 1998.

Perry, Glenn, Ph.D. "Toward a Code of Ethics for Astrologers," *The Mountain Astrologer*, October/November 2001.

Potulin, Ruth. "Astrological Standards and Professional Licensing," *The International Astrologer*, ISAR, Summer 2000.

Soffer, Shirley. "The Ten Rules of Right Behavior for Practicing Astrologers," *NCGR Memberletter*, August 1992.

Wright, Jean. "Mindful, Non-Violent Astrology," *The Mountain Astrologer*, March 1993.

Appendix I:

The NCGR-PAA Code of Ethics

NCGR-PAA's Code of Ethics is adapted in its entirety from NCGR's own Code of Ethics. All candidates for NCGR-PAA testing on any and all Levels and all NCGR-PAA Certified Astrologers are expected to abide by this Code. The current text of the Code of Ethics, published herein, was originally drafted by David Arner and approved by NCGR's Board of Directors in 1998.

Preamble

Astrologers are dedicated to the development and enhancement of the human condition through an understanding of celestial phenomena as applied to human concerns. Astrologers are committed to honesty, fairness and respect for others. Guided by the objective application of astrological technique as well as a commitment to the improvement of the human condition, astrologers seek to increase understanding and compassion worldwide. They remain acutely aware of the need to understand themselves in order to understand and help others.

Astrologers are aware of the immense contribution astrology can make to human knowledge and wisdom, and accordingly encourage inquiry and an open exchange of ideas both outside and within their profession. And above all, astrologers respect the potential power they hold to affect the lives of others, and accordingly strive for the highest levels of competence and diligence.

A. General Standards

    A.1 Applicability of This Code

    A.2 Avoiding Harm

    A.3 Boundaries of Competence

    A.4 Interpretations and Forecasts

A.5 Responsibilities to Others A.6 Human Differences
A.7 Personal Problems and Conflicts
A.8 Sexual Conduct
A.9 Third Party Services

B. Confidentiality

B.1 Maintaining Confidentiality
B.2 Consultations with Colleagues
B.3 Confidential Information in Data Collections

C. Advertising and Public Statements

C.1 Definitions
C.2 False and Deceptive Statements
C.3 Unfounded Statements
C.4 Misuse of Astrology
C.5 Organizational Misrepresentation

D. Business Practices

D.1 Solicitation of Clients
D.2 Boundaries D.3 Referrals D.4 Fees
D.5 General Practices

E. Teaching and Research

E.1 Accuracy and Objectivity
E.2 Active Participation of Subjects
E.3 Crediting and Citing Sources

F. Resolving Ethical Issues

F.1 Confronting Ethical Issues

F.2 Personal and Religious Views

F.3 Cooperating With Ethical Investigations

F.4 Improper Complaints

A. General Standards

A.1 Applicability of This Code

This code applies to the activities of astrologers in their professional work, as well as in their representations and use of astrology at large.

A.2 Avoiding Harm

Astrologers avoid making statements that could cause harm through confusion, misunderstanding or fear.

A.3 Boundaries of Competence

Astrologers provide services to the public whether in astrology or in other disciplines – only within the boundaries of their competence based on their education, training and appropriate experience.

A.4 Interpretations and Forecasts

a. Consulting astrologers are careful to present their astrological interpretations and opinions with objectivity and appropriate qualifying statements, rather than as final or unequivocal pronouncements.

b. Astrologers make predictions only when they are derived from a conscientious application of technique.

A.5 Responsibilities To Others

a. Astrologers respect the rights of others, including clients, students and colleagues, to hold values, attitudes, and opinions different from their own.

b. Astrologers make every effort to refrain from any behavior that may reasonably be considered offensive, harassing or demeaning to others.

c. Consulting astrologers are careful to avoid manipulation of their client's feelings and emotions.

d. Astrologers do not present their interpretations or opinions to their clients in a way that could intimidate them.

A.6 Human Differences

a. Astrologers respect human differences, including those due to astrological configurations, age, gender, race, ethnicity, religion, national origin, disability, sexual gender preference, and socioeconomic status.

b. Should such human differences impair or compromise an astrologer in serving a particular individual or a group, the astrologer makes a conscious effort to ensure fairness and objectivity. Such efforts might include obtaining appropriate training, experience, or advice. Otherwise the astrologer should make an appropriate referral.

A.7 Personal Problems and Conflicts

a. Astrologers refrain from counseling individuals or clients with whom they have personal problems or conflicts which may interfere with their effectiveness or cause harm.

b. Astrologers remain alert to personal problems or conflicts arising during an astrology relationship, and take appropriate measures to correct the situation or to limit, suspend, or terminate the undertaking.

A.8 Sexual Conduct

a. Astrologers do not engage in sexual behavior with clients or students unless such behavior is clearly separate from and outside of the astrological sessions or work.

b. Astrologers do not engage in sexual harassment. Sexual harassment consists of sexual solicitation, physical advances, or any other verbal or non-verbal sexual conduct that is offensive or that the astrologer should realize might be unwelcome. Sexual harassment can take the form of persistent or pervasive acts, or of a single act that is intense or severe.

A.9 Third-Party Services

a. When an astrologer agrees to provide consulting services for someone at the request of another, the astrologer clarifies the role of the astrologer and the extent of and limits to confidentiality with each party.

b. Astrologers do not attempt to manipulate a person's behavior on behalf of a third party.

B. Confidentiality

B.1 Maintaining Confidentiality

a. Astrologers respect the confidentiality and rights to privacy of their clients, students and others who they deal with in astrological contexts. Confidentiality applies to the identity of and personal information about clients and other individuals.

b. Astrologers do not disclose personal information that is unattainable from public sources without the consent of the person involved as long as that person is living.

B.2 Consultations with Colleagues

When consulting with colleagues, astrologers do not share the identity of the person or persons involved without prior consent. If unavoidable, they share only that information which is necessary to achieve the purposes of the consultation.

B.3 Confidential Information in Data Collections

Astrologers seek permission from living subjects (such as clients, students and friends) before including confidential information in named data collections. Alternatively, astrologers use coding or other techniques to protect the identity of the subjects.

C. Advertising and Public Statements

C.1 Definitions

Advertising, whether paid or unpaid, includes all media, such as magazines, newspaper ads, brochures, business cards, fliers and other printed matter, direct mail promotions, directory listings, resumes, etc. Public statements include advertising as well as statements made in classes, lectures, workshops and other oral presentations, published materials, interviews, and comments for use in all electronic media.

C.2 False or Deceptive Statements

a. Astrologers do not make advertising claims or public statements that are false, deceptive, misleading or fraudulent, either because of what they state or suggest, or because of what they omit. This includes claims and statements regarding their training, experience, competence, credentials, organizational affiliations, and services.

b. Astrologers take responsibility for the content of promotional advertising statements made on their behalf.

C.3 Unfounded Statements

Astrologers willingly and openly reveal their sources of information, whether they be scientific, academic, experiential, or mystical. Astrologers do not misrepresent their sources of information, and make every effort to verify their accuracy.

C.4 Misuse of Astrology

a. Misuse includes gross misrepresentation of astrological factors used to make sensational and exaggerated claims in public statements.

b. Astrologers are alert to and guard against personal, financial, social, religious, or political factors that might cause them to misuse their influence.

c. Astrologers do not participate in activities in which it appears likely that their expertise or data will be misused by others.

d. If astrologers learn of the misuse of their work, they take reasonable steps to correct or minimize the misuse or misrepresentation.

C.5 Organizational Misrepresentation

a. NCGR-PAA members who represent themselves as such are careful to clarify whether they are acting as a spokesperson or as an individual.

b. NCGR-PAA members do not act as spokespersons or imply that they are spokespersons for NCGR-PAA without the authorization to do so.

D. Business Practices

D.1 Solicitation of Clients

Astrologers do not make astrological statements, predictions or forecasts in the course of the solicitation of clients or students that are misleading either in their optimism or their negativity, or that are frightening or intimidating.

D.2 Boundaries

Astrologers maintain reasonable boundaries with their clients, with the best interests of their clients in mind.

D.3 Referrals

a. Astrologers make referrals based on the best interests of the client or potential client. Astrologers only recommend other professionals who are to the best of their knowledge qualified, competent, and ethically responsible.

b. Astrologers do not accept referral fees.

D.4 Fees

Astrologers do not exploit recipients of their services with respect to fees, nor do they misrepresent their fees.

D.5 General Practices

a. Astrologers take responsibility for informing their clients of their business practices, such as length and frequency of sessions and kind of work performed.

b. Astrologers make every effort to honor all commitments they have made.

E. Teaching and Research

E.1 Accuracy and Objectivity

When engaged in teaching or writing, astrologers present astrological information accurately and with appropriate objectivity.

E.2 Active Participation of Subjects

In research projects that involve interviews with research subjects, astrologers are careful to consider the negative impact their questions may have on the well-being of those subjects.

E.3 Crediting and Citing Sources

Astrologers realize the importance of intellectual integrity. They are aware that the improper use of copyrighted material is illegal, and that plagiarism (the presentation of another's work as one's own) is dishonest.

F. Resolving Ethical Issues

F.1 Confronting Ethical Issues

Should an astrologer be uncertain how this Ethics Code may apply in a given situation, the astrologer makes a good faith effort to consult with knowledgeable colleagues, organizational representatives, or with other appropriate authorities in order to choose a proper course of action.

F.2 Personal and Religious Views

a. Astrologers whose personal convictions or religious ethics come into conflict with those of a client or student are alert to the possible compromise of objectivity that may arise. In such cases, astrologers clearly separate their views from their astrological interpretations.

b. Astrologers whose personal convictions or religious ethics come into conflict with this code clarify their differences where appropriate.

F.3 Cooperating With Ethics Investigations

a. Astrologers cooperate in ethics investigations, proceedings, and requirements of any organization to which they belong. In doing so, they make reasonable efforts to resolve any issues involving potential breaches of confidentiality.

b. Astrologers are honest in their dealings with ethics bodies. Astrologers do not deceive or withhold appropriate information from ethics bodies.

F.4 Improper Complaints

Astrologers do not file or encourage the filing of ethics complaints that are frivolous and are intended to harm the respondent rather than protect the public.

—Revised October 1998

Applendix II

Calculating a Horoscope

In most situations, calculations are best taught through the dynamic relationship between students and teachers. There are many qualified teachers of calculations in NCGR and in many prestigious astrology schools and organizations. However, these teachers are not always geographically accessible to students embarking on NCGR-PAA's certification program. Calculations are therefore now provided in this Study Guide for those students and for those others who wish to learn Level I calculations through independent study.

The NCGR-PAA exams require basic knowledge of the mechanics of astrological chart (horoscope) calculation. Although astrological charts can be produced instantly by astrological software, we feel that in bypassing manual calculations an understanding of the geophysical and astronomy realities behind the process is lost. A generation of astrologers with no knowledge of how a chart is calculated could limit insight and innovation into the workings of astrology. NCGR-PAA therefore requires some fundamental calculations to be demonstrated on an exam.

An astrological chart, or horoscope (from the Greek horoskopos, "view of the hour"), is a two dimensional map of the sky for a specific day, time, and place. In many respects, it is a circular graph. The sky for astronomers and astrologers is modeled as a celestial sphere. To measure the sky, as seen from the Earth, a grid is projected onto the celestial sphere and points in the sky can then be located relative to points on the grid. Coordinate systems are mathematical projections onto the sky (grids) that allow for precise measurements and graphing of astronomical bodies and points.

Conceptually, the calculation of an astrological chart is simple. Data for planetary positions and the rotation of the Earth are given in tables, usually daily tables. If a birth or an event happens to occur at the time given in the tables, no calculations are necessary. But most births or events happen somewhere between listings in the tables, so to produce most astrological charts, positions between the listings must be calculated by a process called interpolation, where an intermediate position is found between two fixed points. Even at its most complicated, the math for calculating an astrological chart is only on the high school level.

The primary required resource needed for astrological chart calculations is an ephemeris (see below). An ephemeris is a daily listing of planetary positions for a specific time of day (usually midnight or noon) at a specific location (usually Greenwich, England where the Royal Observatory is located). The positions of the planets are given in celestial longitude, and often also in celestial latitude and declination. Because the precise latitude and longitude of a birth or event is required for an accurate astrological chart, an atlas with latitudes, longitudes and information on time changes for cities and towns is another needed resource. In addition, a table of houses is useful for determining house cusps, though these calculations can also be done without such tables. Other tools may include tables for interpolating planetary positions, a four function calculator (or a scientific

Solar Fire v8.0.3

GMT +0:00 Tropical Geocentric Long	Moon ☽	Sun ☉	Mercury ☿	Venus ♀	Mars ♂	Jupiter ♃	Saturn ♄	Uranus ♅	Neptune ♆	Pluto ♇
May 1 2008	09°♓53'	10°♉59'	26°♉45'	00°♉32'	25°♋19'	22°♑15'	01°♍41' ℞	21°♓24'	24°♒04'	00°♑56' ℞
May 2 2008	23°♓37'	11°♉58'	28°♉32'	01°♉45'	25°♋50'	22°♑16'	01°♍40'	21°♓26'	24°♒05'	00°♑55'
May 3 2008	07°♈51'	12°♉56'	00°♊17'	02°♉59'	26°♋22'	22°♑18'	01°♍40'	21°♓29'	24°♒06'	00°♑54'
May 4 2008	22°♈32'	13°♉54'	01°♊58'	04°♉13'	26°♋53'	22°♑19'	01°♍40' D	21°♓31'	24°♒06'	00°♑53'
May 5 2008	07°♉34'	14°♉52'	03°♊35'	05°♉27'	27°♋25'	22°♑20'	01°♍40'	21°♓33'	24°♒07'	00°♑52'
May 6 2008	22°♉48'	15°♉50'	05°♊09'	06°♉41'	27°♋57'	22°♑20'	01°♍41'	21°♓36'	24°♒08'	00°♑51'
May 7 2008	08°♊04'	16°♉48'	06°♊38'	07°♉55'	28°♋28'	22°♑21'	01°♍41'	21°♓38'	24°♒08'	00°♑50'
May 8 2008	23°♊09'	17°♉46'	08°♊04'	09°♉09'	29°♋00'	22°♑21'	01°♍42'	21°♓40'	24°♒09'	00°♑49'
May 9 2008	07°♋56'	18°♉44'	09°♊26'	10°♉23'	29°♋32'	22°♑22'	01°♍42'	21°♓43'	24°♒10'	00°♑48'
May 10 2008	22°♋18'	19°♉42'	10°♊44'	11°♉36'	00°♌04'	22°♑22' ℞	01°♍43'	21°♓45'	24°♒10'	00°♑47'
May 11 2008	06°♌13'	20°♉40'	11°♊58'	12°♉50'	00°♌37'	22°♑21'	01°♍44'	21°♓47'	24°♒11'	00°♑46'
May 12 2008	19°♌42'	21°♉38'	13°♊08'	14°♉04'	01°♌09'	22°♑21'	01°♍45'	21°♓49'	24°♒11'	00°♑45'
May 13 2008	02°♍48'	22°♉36'	14°♊13'	15°♉18'	01°♌41'	22°♑20'	01°♍46'	21°♓51'	24°♒12'	00°♑44'
May 14 2008	15°♍33'	23°♉34'	15°♊14'	16°♉32'	02°♌14'	22°♑20'	01°♍47'	21°♓53'	24°♒12'	00°♑43'
May 15 2008	28°♍03'	24°♉32'	16°♊11'	17°♉45'	02°♌46'	22°♑19'	01°♍48'	21°♓55'	24°♒13'	00°♑42'
May 16 2008	10°♎20'	25°♉30'	17°♊03'	18°♉59'	03°♌19'	22°♑18'	01°♍49'	21°♓57'	24°♒13'	00°♑41'
May 17 2008	22°♎28'	26°♉28'	17°♊51'	20°♉13'	03°♌52'	22°♑16'	01°♍51'	21°♓59'	24°♒13'	00°♑39'
May 18 2008	04°♏30'	27°♉26'	18°♊34'	21°♉27'	04°♌24'	22°♑15'	01°♍52'	22°♓01'	24°♒14'	00°♑38'
May 19 2008	16°♏27'	28°♉23'	19°♊13'	22°♉40'	04°♌57'	22°♑13'	01°♍54'	22°♓03'	24°♒14'	00°♑37'
May 20 2008	28°♏21'	29°♉21'	19°♊47'	23°♉54'	05°♌30'	22°♑11'	01°♍55'	22°♓04'	24°♒14'	00°♑36'
May 21 2008	10°♐14'	00°♊19'	20°♊16'	25°♉08'	06°♌03'	22°♑09'	01°♍57'	22°♓06'	24°♒14'	00°♑34'
May 22 2008	22°♐06'	01°♊16'	20°♊41'	26°♉22'	06°♌36'	22°♑07'	01°♍59'	22°♓08'	24°♒14'	00°♑33'
May 23 2008	04°♑00'	02°♊14'	21°♊00'	27°♉35'	07°♌09'	22°♑04'	02°♍01'	22°♓10'	24°♒15'	00°♑32'
May 24 2008	15°♑58'	03°♊12'	21°♊15'	28°♉49'	07°♌43'	22°♑02'	02°♍03'	22°♓11'	24°♒15'	00°♑30'
May 25 2008	28°♑02'	04°♊09'	21°♊25'	00°♊03'	08°♌16'	21°♑59'	02°♍05'	22°♓13'	24°♒15'	00°♑29'
May 26 2008	10°♒17'	05°♊07'	21°♊31'	01°♊17'	08°♌49'	21°♑56'	02°♍08'	22°♓14'	24°♒15'	00°♑28'
May 27 2008	22°♒46'	06°♊05'	21°♊32' ℞	02°♊30'	09°♌23'	21°♑53'	02°♍10'	22°♓16'	24°♒15' ℞	00°♑26'
May 28 2008	05°♓34'	07°♊02'	21°♊28'	03°♊44'	09°♌56'	21°♑50'	02°♍13'	22°♓17'	24°♒15'	00°♑25'
May 29 2008	18°♓44'	08°♊00'	21°♊20'	04°♊58'	10°♌30'	21°♑46'	02°♍15'	22°♓19'	24°♒15'	00°♑24'
May 30 2008	02°♈22'	08°♊57'	21°♊07'	06°♊12'	11°♌04'	21°♑43'	02°♍18'	22°♓20'	24°♒15'	00°♑22'

Applendix II

calculator that converts degrees into decimals and vice versa), logarithmic or trigonometric tables, and pencil and paper.

There are at least four methods of calculating an astrological chart. All will produce the same results if done properly. These are listed below.

1. Interpolation from tables. Before computers this was the method most astrologers in the 20th century used to calculate house cusps and planetary positions. Calculating an astrological chart from tables is somewhat convenient and not particularly difficult. It can, however, be time-consuming and requires several detailed tables for utmost accuracy.

2. Calculating by proportions. This method is similar to that above except that it does not use intermediate tables of any kind to locate planetary positions or house cusps. It uses arithmetic for a few simple calculations that convert the time of birth to a proportion of the day and then it applies this fraction to ephemeris planetary positions. Likewise, house cusp positions are calculated proportionally from a table of houses which gives the cusps for specific degrees of latitude and sidereal time. These operations can be expressed as algebraic formulae. Those comfortable with simple equations and conversions back and forth between sexigesimal notation and decimals will be able to do these calculations rapidly on a calculator.

3. Logarithms. The word logarithm means a number that indicates a ratio. This method, which turns multiplication and division into addition and subtraction, was first developed and published in the early 17th century by the mathematician John Napier and was used intensively by Joannes Kepler. For centuries astrologers used logarithms to facilitate astrological chart calculations. A table of logarithms is required to find ratios, and then to reverse interpolate and find numbers.

4. Trigonometry. Since astrological charts are two-dimensional representations of a three-dimensional reality depicted as a celestial sphere, the mathematical tool of choice for locating points on the celestial sphere is trigonometry. Using only an ephemeris and atlas, the components of an astrological chart can be calculated with only a few formulae and some proportional adjustments. For those comfortable with such things, this is by far the fastest and most accurate method of calculating a chart, but it requires a scientific calculator. In the past, trigonometric tables were used for these calculations.

The Astronomy Behind Chart Calculations

Astrological chart calculations are based on scientific data and there is only one correct chart for any set of birth data. The location of each of the planets is the same for anywhere on Earth and is given in the ephemeris for each day, month by month, year by year. The rotation of Earth is given in what is called sidereal time (time based upon the rotation of Earth with reference to the background of stars), which allows for the calculation of the house cusps.

The Earth rotates on its axis once each day, all the while moving along its orbit around the Sun each year. Consequently, astronomical positions change on a daily basis. The Sun does not rise at the same time every day because of the yearly orbit and these changes must be compensated for when calculating an astrological chart. It is recommended that an understanding of coordinate systems and the rotation of the Earth be understood through diagrams and computer simulations before learning to calculate an astrological chart.

Unfortunately, many astrologers become so attached to their ephemerides or computers that they don't know where to look in the sky for a planet even if they know the planet's sign and degree. We encourage exam takers to get outside at night away from cities whenever possible and make an effort to see planets and obtain a visual understanding of zodiacal positions. An alternate method of developing a sense of sky in relation to the astrological chart is to use computer planetarium programs. Bear in mind, however, that in Western astrology most use the Tropical Zodiac, but in astronomy the Sidereal Zodiac is more often used.

The Basic Calculations

Regardless of what method one uses to calculate an astrological chart, the following calculations are preliminary. First, it is necessary to understand that time is expressed locally (Local Sidereal Time – LST) and must be adjusted and also converted to time at Greenwich, England (Greenwich Mean Time – GMT). Since the Earth rotates 360 degrees a day, but at the same time is orbiting the Sun (which means that the astronomical time of noon will change by about 4 minutes each day), a solar-sidereal correction must be applied.

A simple way to determine the solar-sidereal correction (SSC, also called the acceleration correction) on the GMT is to use tables. Another is to divide the GMT by 6.1. Express the GMT in decimals, divide that figure by 6.1 and then divide the result by 60 (which configures the result to minutes and seconds).

Calculations of planetary positions involve working with degrees, minutes and seconds. Calculations of house cusps involve working with hours and minutes. In both cases the base is 60 (sexagesimal numeration). Degrees are indicated the degree symbol °, minutes by ' and seconds by ". (Note: there are 60 seconds in a minute and 60 minutes in a degree.)

Chart calculations involve modular arithmetic. For example, when working with sexigesimal notation it is necessary to make corrections to figures over 60. Eg., 65 minutes equals 1 degree and 5 minutes, 60 being the modulus in this case. The same principle applies to 24 hours. If a calculation results in a GMT of 29 hours and 15 minutes, this becomes 5 hours and 15 minutes into the next day.

> Example: Adding and subtracting in sexigesimal notation requires understanding that minutes and seconds can never be more than 59. If in a calculation either are 60 or higher, you must subtract sixty and increase the next higher unit by one step. For example, if the number of minutes found in a calculation amounts to 73, then you must subtract 60,

leaving 13 as the number of minutes – but the number of degrees will increase by 1. Here's a specific example:

$$13° \ 32' \ 45''$$
$$+ \ 14° \ 18' \ 39''$$
$$= 27° \ 50' \ 84''$$

As 84 in the seconds column is greater than 60, subtract 60 to get 24" and add one minute to the minutes column.

The result is now 27° 51' 24"

When working with time, which is a major part of chart calculating, the degree column is hours. The above figure would read 27 hours, 51 minutes and 24 seconds. Since there are 24 hours in a day and no more, 24 must be subtracted from 27 and the result is then 3 hours 51 minutes and 24 seconds – but now the figure carries over to the next day.

Some prefer to work in the sexigesimal system as described above, others prefer to change degrees, minutes and seconds, or hour and minutes, to a decimal which then facilitates calculations. This is easily done on a scientific calculator (note: each manufacturer has its own specific key sequence for this conversion). Conversions can also be done on a standard calculator using the following sequences.

To convert degrees/minutes/seconds to decimals:

Seconds ÷ 60 = + minutes = ÷ 60 = + degrees =

To convert decimals to degrees/minutes/seconds (degrees are always shown left of decimal point):

Subtract degrees and begin with decimals only. Multiply this figure by 60 = minutes (digits left of decimal point). Subtract minutes and multiply the remaining decimals by 60 = seconds.

Astrological calculations require that the location of the birth or event be part of the calculation, and thus require the longitude and latitude of the location, which requires an atlas or some other means of accessing this data. Calculations for house cusps, which include the Ascendan and Midheaven, are usually done using a table of houses. These tables usually list house cusps in various systems for a wide range of latitudes, and in some cases for specific cities. Note that house cusp calculations can be done without using a table of houses, though these calculations will vary in complexity depending on the house system used. The Porphyry house system does not require a table of houses for the intermediate house cusps as it is based on the trisection of the arcs between the Midheaven and Ascendant axes. Please note that NCGR-PAA accepts calculations of house cusps in any system except the following: equal house and whole-sign houses.

Worksheet for Preliminary Calculations (for all methods)

Basic Chart Data:

Name/Event _____

Year _____ Month _____ Day _____

Time _____ AM - PM

Time (24 hour time) _____

Location _____

Time Zone _____

Latitude _____ Longitude _____

Worksheet for Calculations using Proportions and Decimal Conversions

The following worksheets outline a method of horoscope calculation that requires a midnight ephemeris, a table of houses and a scientific calculator. This relatively simple procedure finds the required data by proportioning which is facilitated greatly by conversions from degrees, minutes and seconds to decimals – and the reverse. Alternatively, the same steps can be followed using house cusp interpolation tables and tables of diurnal planetary motion.

A. Finding the Greenwich Mean Time (GMT) (also called the Universal Time (UT):

1. Local Standard Time (24 h time) _____ h _____ m _____ s
2. Daylight/War Time correction: _____ h _____ _____
3. Subtract 2 from 1: _____ h _____ m _____ s
4. Time zone adjustment (+W/-E) _____ h
5. Add 3 & 4:
Result = Greenwich Mean Time: _____ h _____ m _____ s
   GMT)
(if over 24, subtract 24 and use _____ h _____ m _____ s
the following day for #1 below)
   Adjusted day _____

Example: *May 5, 2008 at 11:57 AM, Boston MA.*

(11:57 local time) – (1 hour DT) + Zone (5) = 15:57 (expressed in decimals, = 15.95). This is the GMT.

Summary:

Birth Time corrected for DT or WT, +/- Time Zone = GMT

Note: a time correction called Delta T (difference between ephemeris time and astronomical time) may be added. This correction is minor and should be included if great accuracy is required. In 1950 the correction was +30 seconds, in 2000 it was +66 seconds.

Applendix II

B. Finding the Local Sidereal Time (LST) with a **midnight** ephemeris:

1. Sidereal Time (ST) from ephemeris: _____h_____m_____s
2. + Greenwich Mean Time: _____h_____m_____s
3. + solar-sidereal correction (SSC)
   (GMT ÷ 6.1) _____m_____s
4. Add 1, 2, and 3: _____h_____m_____s
5. Longitude time equivalent (LTE): _____h_____m_____s
   (longitude ÷ 15)
6. Subtract 5 from 4 if west longitude,
   add 5 to 4 if east long.
   (Add 24 to #4 if figure is too small for subtraction)
   _____h_____m_____s
7. Result: Local Sidereal Time (LST) _____h_____m_____s

Example:

1. ST = 14:52:57 (converted to decimals is 14.8825)
2. + 15:57 GMT (15.95 in decimals)
3. + SSC = 0:02:37 GMT ÷ (divided by) 6.1 and then by 60 = 0.0435.)
4. = 29:112:94 or 30:52:34. (30.876 in decimals)
5. LTE = 4:44:14. (long. = 71:03:37, from tables LTE = 4:44:14)
   (or convert to decimals – 71.0603 ÷ 15 = 4.7374)
6. #5 minus #4: 30:52:34 – 4:44:14 = 26:08:20
   (in decimals 30.876 – 4.7374 = 26.1386)
   Subtract 24 = 2.1386 or 2:08:18)
7. LST = 2:08:18

Summary:

ST + GMT + SSC – LTE = LST

Note: *For births in the Southern Hemisphere, add 12 hours to L.S.T. and add 180° to the listed house cusps if calculated from a standard table of houses.*

Calculating house cusps using a table of houses

After calculating the GMT and LST as previously explained, you will need to calculate the Midheaven, Ascendant, house cusps and planets, in that order. Except for the Porphyry house system which can be calculated directly, a table of houses is required for this method. There is some variation among tables of houses. Some list sidereal times and house cusps for specific latitudes, usually large cities. Others list sidereal times at four minute intervals, still others list midheavens at one degree intervals. In any case, the problem is one of finding exactly where your calculated LST fits in with the given data (except in rare instances when the calculated LST is the same as a listed ST).

The math problems required in finding the house cusps involves basic arithmetic; addition, subtraction, multiplication and division. House cusp interpolation tables, such as those found in the *Michelsen Book of Tables*, may be helpful to those who are uncomfortable with arithmetic. Most horoscope calculations are facilitated by the use of a scientific calculator with which one can easily convert degrees, minutes and seconds (sexagesimal notation) to decimals. The calculations can then be done in decimals and reconverted later when the data is placed in the horoscope. Important – not all calculators are the same and routines differ. Read your calculators manual and practice conversions before attempting to calculate a horoscope.

C. Calculating the Midheaven

Previously calculated LST: _____h _____m _____s

In a table of houses locate the sidereal time listings, one lesser and one greater, that are nearest to the calculated LST. In most cases your calculated LST will fall between these two listed sidereal times. In some tables of houses, the listed sidereal times will be exactly four minutes apart, in others the midheaven positions will be spaced exactly one degree apart. Which is better is a matter of preference. Use the following formula to calculate the Midheaven or cusp of the tenth house. If possible, convert to decimals, work the problem, then reconvert.

Applendix II

A Sample Table of Houses

Sidereal Time:	2h 07m 00s				
Midheaven:	4° Taurus				
Cusps:	11	12	1	2	3
Latitude 42 N:	17Ge14	17Ca55	14Le51	11Vi00	7Li34
Latitude 43 N:	17Ge48	18cA28	15lE07	11vI18	7Li43

Sidereal Time:	2h 10m 52s				
Midheaven:	5° Taurus				
Cusps:	11	12	1	2	3
Latitude 42 N:	18Ge00	18Ca37	15Le26	11Vi50	8Li30
Latitude 43 N:	18Ge34	19Ca09	15Le52	12Vi08	8Li38

Here is a section from a typical table of houses that is pertinent to the example used below. In this case the Midheaven (house 10) is given in whole degrees and the houses in degrees and minutes. The Ascendant is house 1, houses 5 through 9 are opposite the ones calculated.

Subtract the lesser ST (from the table of houses) from your calculated LST.

1. Calculated LST _____h _____m _____s
   Minus Lesser ST _____h _____m _____s from table of houses
   = _____m _____s

2. Difference between given greater and lesser ST from table of houses

   Greater ST _____h _____m _____s
   Minus lesser ST _____h _____m _____s
   = _____m _____s

3. Convert results to decimals on calculator and divide #1 by #2. This can also be done by first converting #1 and #2 into seconds, then

NCGR-PAA Study Guide

dividing. The result (four decimal places is enough) will be a fraction. (Save this figure as you will need it to calculate the other house cusps.)

#1 divided by #2 = _____

4. Subtract the difference between the two midheavens given in the table of houses for the two sidereal times you have been working with and multiply this figure by #3.

later midheaven	____d	____m	____s
earlier midheaven	____d	____m	____s
=	____d	____m	____s
x (#3)	_____		
=	_____		

5. Reconvert result to degrees/minutes/seconds. Add the result of #4 to the earlier midheaven to obtain the exact midheaven you are seeking.

#4 in degrees	____d	____m	____s
+ earlier midheaven	____d	____m	____s
= calculated midheaven	____d	____m	____s

Example:

Previously calculated LST = 2:08:18 (in decimals 2.1386)

1. *Calculated LST minus lesser LST: 2:08:18 − 2:07:00 = 0:01:18*
2. *Difference between greater and lesser ST from tables:*
   2:10:52 − 2:07:00 = 0:03:52
3. *Use interpolation tables or convert above to decimals and divide #1 by #2:*
   0.0217 ÷ 0.0644 = 0.3370
4. *Difference between listed Midheavens: 5 − 4 = 1,*
   multiply by #3 = 0.3370
5. *Convert result back to d m s and add to earlier Midheaven: 0d 20m 13s + 4 = 4 Taurus 20*

D. Calculating the Ascendant

Previously Calculated LST _____d _____m _____s

Fraction (decimals) from step C#3 above _____

The latitude for the birth or event must be taken into account when calculating the Ascendant and intermediate house cusps. The calculation of the Ascendant and the intermediate house cusps exactly requires three operations. Because most tables of houses only give house cusps for round number latitudes, Ascendants and house cusps for the nearest lesser and nearest greater latitudes must first be calculated. Only then can the Ascendant and house cusps for the exact latitude of the birth or event be determined. Note that you will only need to calculate cusps for houses 11, 12, 1 (Ascendant), 2 and 3. The others are exactly opposite in the zodiac.

House cusps can be calculated by several methods including solving the problem with proportions as outlined below, with logarithms or by using interpolation tables. This is a matter of preference, the results will be the same. Although the calculations will use degrees, minutes and seconds, the final results can omit seconds and be rounded to the nearest minutes. The following steps are based on the example house tables on page 141. Other tables of houses may differ and may be handled best by first calculating cusps for lesser and greater latitudes at the LST, then calculating for the exact latitude.

Ascendant calculations for the geographical latitude

1. Determine the difference between the nearest lesser latitude and the nearest greater latitude. This is often 1 degree.

Nearest greater latitude _____d _____m _____s
Nearest lesser latitude _____d _____m _____s
          =   _____d _____m _____s

2. Determine the difference between the given latitude and the nearest lesser latitude:

Given latitude	_____d	_____m	_____s
Nearest lesser latitude	_____d	_____m	_____s
=	_____d	_____m	_____s

3. Convert to decimals and divide the result of #2 by the result of #1. This fraction will be used for the calculation of each intermediate house cusp.

#2 / #1 = _____

4. Determine the difference between the Ascendant listings at the nearest lesser and nearest greater latitudes for the lesser sidereal time. (Note: Ascendants may increase or decrease with latitude depending on sidereal time.) Express this difference in minutes of arc.

	_____d	_____m	_____s
	_____d	_____m	_____s
Difference =	_____d	_____m	_____s

Difference expressed in minutes _____

5. Multiply this difference by D#3 above. Then add (or subtract, see above) this figure to the Ascendant listing at the at the nearest lesser latitude.

Difference_____x #3_____ = _____m _____s
Add (or subtract) to lesser latitude
_____d _____m _____s
= Calculated Ascendant for
lesser sidereal time   _____d _____m _____s

6. Do the same calculations for the greater sidereal time. This is the Ascendant for the required latitude at the nearest greater sidereal time.

Applendix II

Difference _____ x #3 _____ = _____ m _____ s
Add (or subtract) to lesser latitude
　　　　　　　　　　　 _____ d _____ m _____ s
= Calculated Ascendant for
greater sidereal time 　　 _____ d _____ m _____ s

7. You now have two Ascendants for the latitude you want, but at two sidereal times. Calculate the difference between these two figures and multiply the result by the fraction from step C#3 used for calculating the Midheaven.

Ascendant for lesser sidereal time 　_____ d _____ m _____ s
Ascendant for greater sidereal time _____ d _____ m _____ s
　　=　　Difference _____ d _____ m _____ s
　　x　　fraction 　_____ = _____

8. Add the result to the lesser Ascendant and you will have the exact Ascendant for the required latitude.

Lesser Ascendant 　　_____ d _____ m _____ s
+ Result of #7 　　　 _____ d _____ m _____ s
　　=　　　　　　　 _____ d _____ m _____ s = Ascendant

Example:

1. Difference between nearest lesser and greater latitudes: 43 – 42 = 1 degree

2. Difference between required latitude (42:21:30) and lesser latitude (42) = 0:21:30

3. Convert to decimals and divide #2 by #1: 0.3583 ÷ 1 = 0.3583

4. Difference between Ascendants for lesser sidereal time: 15:07:00 – 14:41:00 = 0:26:00　　(0.4333 in decimals)

5. Multiply by #4 by #3: 0.3583 x 0.4333 = 0.1553 or 0:09:19. Add to Ascendant for lesser latitude: 14:41:00 + 0:09:19 = 14:50:19 (roughly 14 Leo 50)

6. Do the same for the greater sidereal time: 15:52:00 − 15:26:00 = 0:26:00 (0.4333 in decimals). 0.4333 x 0.3583 = 0.1553 = 0:09:19. 15:26:00 + 0:09:19 = 15:35:19 (roughly 15 Leo 35).

7. Difference between Ascendants at lesser and greater latitudes: 15:35:19 − 14:50:19 = 0:45:19 (0.7553 in decimals). Multiply by 0.3370 from Midheaven calculation: C#3

8. Add to lesser Ascendant: 14:50:19 + 0:15:14 = 15:05:33 (roughly 15 Leo 6).

E. Calculating the Houses

After calculating an exact Midheaven and Ascendant, and placing them in the proper positions on a chart form, the intermediate houses cusps (houses 11, 12, 2 and 3) must be added. To calculate the intermediate houses cusps exactly use the worksheet for the Ascendant above but substitute each house cusp for the Ascendant. (Porphyry houses, which are trisections of each quadrant, do not require a table of houses and can be done easily on a calculator.)

Summary:

For both lesser and greater sidereal times:

1. Calculate each house cusp for the nearest lesser latitude.
2. Calculate each house cusp for the nearest greater latitude.
3. Calculate each house cusp for the actual latitude.

Use the fraction from Midheaven calculation #3 to find the house cusp you want.

Calculated house cusps (12, 11, 1, 2, 3) should be placed at appropriate places on a standard astrological chart form. Opposite houses will have the same degrees as calculated but opposite zodiacal signs. Intercepted signs may be written between houses where needed.

F. Calculation of the planets' longitudes

Formula: Planet's daily motion x Constant Fraction = distance traveled. To this add the planet's previous ephemeris listing. This equals the planet's position at the GMT.

Determining the Constant Fraction:

1. GMT: _____ h _____ m _____ s
   GMT date: _____

2. Express minutes and seconds of GMT in decimal form:
   _____ (to 4 or 5 places)

3. Divide by 24 = _____. This is the Constant Fraction (CF). Store this figure in calculator's memory. Remember that in some cases the GMT of birth or the event will fall into the next day.

Example:

1. GMT = 15:57
2. GMT in decimals = 15.95
3. Divide GMT by 24: 15.95 ÷ 24 = 0.6646 (constant fraction)

Planet position calculations use the constant fraction to locate where in each planet's daily motion it was for the time of the event or birth. The daily motion is found by subtracting the earlier position (normally the day of the event or birth) from the later position (the next day). Note that this will be the reverse for retrograde planets. If the planet's degree of longitude after calculation is over 30, subtract 30. Computation of planetary positions can also be done using tables of diurnal motion of the planets.

Note: In the case of the Sun and Moon, the daily motion is normally given in degrees, minutes, and seconds to facilitate calculations for solar and lunar returns. For natal charts, this level of precision is not necessary. Planet positions do not require calculations to the second.

NCGR-PAA Study Guide

1. Later ephemeris position: _____d _____m
2. Previous ephemeris position _____d _____m
3. Subtract 2 from 1 to obtain daily motion (add if retrograde). _____d _____m
4. Convert to decimals: _____ = Daily Motion
5. Multiply daily motion (DM) by the Constant Fraction (CF) to determine distance traveled (DT):
   DM _____ x CF_____ = _____
6. Convert DT to degrees and minutes: _____d _____m
7. Add previous position (line 2): _____d _____m
8. Equals planet's longitude: _____d _____m

in sign _____

Adjust zodiacal sign if necessary:

Example

> (Sun position for event on May 5th, 2008 – see ephemeris on page132):
> 1. Later ephemeris position = 15 Ta 50
> 2. Earlier ephemeris position = 14 Ta 52
> 3. Daily motion = 0 d 58 m
> 4. Convert to decimals = 0.9667
> 5. Daily motion x constant fraction: 0.9667 x 0.6646 = 0.64245
> 6. Convert to d m s = 0d 38m 33s
> 7. Add to planet's earlier position: 14 Ta 52 + 38m 33s = 15 Ta 30 and 33s
> 8. Longitude of Sun = 15 Ta 31 (round up the 33 seconds to the next degree)

Do the same procedure for the Moon and the other planets. After all planetary positions have been calculated, place them in the circular horoscope form with previously calculated house cusps.

Appendix III

The History of Astrology

The Ancient Middle East

Mesopotamia (today's Iraq and northeast Syria) was the birthplace of Western astrology. In this region some 4,000 years or more ago astrology evolved as a highly developed omen system utilized by a series of civilizations. It is thought that the unstable natural and political environment of the Mesopotamian region encouraged the development of a predictive system such as astrology. Mesopotamian astrology was not horoscopic; that is, it did not involve the casting of specific charts erected for a definite time, place, and date, as is done for birthcharts in modern practice. It was an omen-based astrology, meant for kings and princes of the region, that emphasized the conjunctions, oppositions, risings, settings, and first and last visibilities of the planets and their correlations with natural phenomena and political events.

Records of astrological interpretations are found on thousands of cuneiform tablets. The earliest currently known astrological records are the Ammizaduga tablets (first Babylonian dynasty, 1645-1625 BC) which contain information on the phases of the planet Venus. The earliest known horoscope from this region dates to 410 BC.

The stable and continuous Egyptian civilization, centered along the Nile River, was less pessimistic and fearful in outlook than in the region of Mesopotamia. The Egyptian relationship to the stars took the forms of astral-religion and sophistication in time-keeping, rather than prognostication. The temples in Egypt show precise astronomical alignments. Calendar science was highly developed and eventually influenced the rest of the world. The most important astronomical event in ancient Egypt was the heliacal rising of Sirius which coincided with the flooding of the Nile, a regular and completely predictable occurrence. (See also the section on Mesopotamian astrology in the non-Western astrology section later on in this Appendix.)

Greece and Rome

Following the conquests of Alexander the Great, Middle Eastern ideas on astrology spread to Greece and India. The mixing of Greek geometry with Mesopotamian astrology, during what is called the Hellenistic Period, produced an elaborate body of information on horoscope reading. A significant contributor to this synthesis was Berossus, a Chaldean, who taught the Greeks astrology at his school in Cos around 280 BC. Later, Egypt emerged as the great center of astrological studies, a factor which tended to obscure astrology's earlier Mesopotamian origins. One of the earliest, and certainly the best known, astrological manual of this period was attributed to Nechepso-Petosiris, a king and his priest, in the 2nd century B.C. The oldest known work on horary and electional astrology (circa 75 AD) was written by Dorotheus of Sidon.

The Greeks also furthered the development of astronomy by speculating on the physical nature of the solar system. Ptolemy, a Greek living in Alexandria, Egypt (c.100-c.150 AD), has been considered the greatest scientist of the ancient world. His writings encompassed astronomy, geography, optics, and several other subjects. Ptolemy also wrote a short work on astrology, the *Tetrabiblos*, as well as the mathematically dense *Almagest*, an astronomical text that argued for a geocentric universe. Both books influenced Western thinking on astrology and astronomy for the next 1,500 years.

Contemporary with Ptolemy was Vettius Valens of Antioch (120-c.175 AD), a working astrologer who wrote a major work on astrology titled the *Anthology*. Unlike the scientific tone of Ptolemy's writings, Valens work is more of a casebook of applied astrology.

The Roman Empire was fertile ground for the spreading of astrology. By the time of Augustus, astrology had infiltrated nearly every aspect of Roman life. It was during this era that the poet Manilius wrote his epic poem on astrology, the *Astronomicon*. From time to time, however, charlatan astrologers filled the streets of Rome offering curbside readings. Other astrologers made predictions of when the emperor would die. These excesses led to the passing of laws to regulate the practice of astrology and also to mass expulsions of astrologers and other fortune tellers from Rome.

On a more serious level, the popular philosophy of Stoicism accepted and supported astrology. Stoicism was a philosophy of life which many leading Romans embraced, including Roman notables Cicero and Seneca. Stoic moral philosophy taught acceptance of one's fate and Stoic metaphysics offered an explanation for the workings of astrology in a scientific sense. Astrology also reached to the highest social levels in Rome. At least two emperors were deeply involved in the subject: Tiberius employed it on a grand scale and Hadrian practiced it himself. Many consulting astrologers were among the most learned men of the time.

Toward the later part of the Roman Empire, Firmicus Maternus (280-360 AD), a lawyer and senator, wrote the *Mathesis*, a textbook on the subject, most of which is still intact. In 378 AD, just a few years after Maternus, Paulus of Alexandria wrote the *Introduction*, another summary of the astrological knowledge of Roman times.

The Middle Ages

The Islamic conquests brought a new political order to the Middle East and North Africa. Cultural centers such as Baghdad preserved and cultivated subjects, including astrology. In general, the Arab civilization of the Middle Ages preserved Greek and Roman astrology and improved on certain aspects of it. Arabic astrology was eclectic, mundane (historical) and mathematical. The astrology of individuals, however, was not well represented. Electional, horary, and medical astrology were emphasized, thus avoiding conflicts with religious ideas on fatalism.

Among the many influential Arabic astrologers were Abu Mashar (c.787-886 AD), a leading court astrologer who was said to have authored fifty books. He is known for his book *Introduction to Astrology* and his writings on mundane astrology and on solar returns. Other leading Arabic astrologers were AlKindi (c. 796-873 AD), a prolific philosophical writer on astrology, and Al-Biruni (c. 973-1048 AD) a universal scholar who was also an astronomer.

In Medieval Europe astrology as a discipline was barely preserved as an integrated body of knowledge. Early Christianity regarded astrology as pagan and discouraged its study and practice. The decline and loss of cultural centers also kept astrological interest at a very low level. Ultimately, Christian theology came to the position that natural astrology (astro-meteorology, plant and medical astrology, etc.) was entirely legitimate, but judicial astrology (natal, electional, and horary) posed some very serious problems in regard to free-will and a person's relationship to God. Judicial astrology was discouraged, if not clearly outlawed.

By the 13th century the situation had changed. Most Italian courts had astrologers and the subject was being taught at the universities. The influx of Arab translations of Greek and Roman astrological works was an important element in this resurgence of interest. The astrologer Campanus (1233-1296), associated with a house system named for him, lived during this period and was a respected astronomer as well.

The theologian Thomas Aquinas, in his book *Summa Contra Gentiles*, addressed the free-will issue in astrology by stating that human mastery of the emotions can overcome the influence of the stars. Guido Bonatti (1194-1250) was one of the outstanding astrologers of the time. He taught at the University of Bologna, wrote a major textbook on astrology and, as a consultant, had many high-ranking clients.

The Renaissance

The revival of interest in antiquity fueled an interest in astrology. Philosophical traditions of the ancient Greek and Roman cultures such as Hermeticism and Neoplatonism that supported astrology were revived and became influential. Marsilio Ficino was a leader in the translation of Arabic texts on astrology and related subjects and is now seen as a pioneer in astrological personality theory.

Printing was part of a process (the rise of the middle class) that enabled a much larger class of people to patronize astrologers. Printing also enabled a much wider dissemination of astrological concepts and tools, especially through almanacs. At this same time events such as the publication of Pico della Mirandola's massive attack on astrology in 1497 and a rash of failed predictions of a great flood in 1524 served to discredit astrology. (According to Lynn Thorndike's *History of Magic and Experimental Science*, 1524 was a very wet year, indeed, and there was much flood damage. The problem was that many astrologers, competing with each other for attention, had predicted a Noah-type flood—which of course did not happen.) Further problems came from the Protestant movement, particularly from John Calvin, which was hostile to astrology.

However, astrology still managed to play a major role in the thought, science and politics of the period. Jerome Cardan (1501-1576) was a true Renaissance man—a famous intellectual and a successful astrologer. Valentin Naibod (1527-1593) authored a general treatise on astrology and advocated a measure of time used in forecasting that is named for him. Dr. John Dee (1527-1608), an English astrologer and scientist, served Queen Elizabeth I as an advisor.

The Scientific Revolution

During the late Renaissance a powerful intellectual movement began, known at the time as experimental science. It developed out of what was called natural philosophy and was essentially a new, democratic way of producing useful knowledge. Stimulated by the rise of trade and the need to solve practical problems, it went on to become the dominant thought system of the modern world. Many of the pioneers and founders of modern science were also astrologers or were generally friendly toward astrology. Of these, the best known are Tycho Brahe (1534-1588) and Johannes Kepler (1571-1630). Galileo (1564-1642) did in fact cast some astrological charts, but he was also skeptical of astrology. However, the progressive nature of the scientific revolution initiated by these individuals and others quickly destroyed the Aristotelian and Ptolemaic systems, both of which served to rationalize and validate astrology.

The transition from the premodern to modern science began in 1543 when Copernicus proposed that Earth revolves around the sun. Later, Kepler refined Copernicus' system, Galileo showed that there were more things in space than could be seen with the naked eye, and

Newton extended the application of mathematics to physical phenomena large and small. The predictions made by these scientists, who at first limited their subject matter to astronomy, physics, ballistics, and optics, could not be argued with, unlike the predictions made by their contemporary astrologers. While new and convincing scientific explanations for natural phenomena were emerging, astrologers failed to organize or agree upon anything, thus insuring themselves of failure in the eyes of the new establishment

The English Tradition

While astrology and astronomy were separating in the 17th and 18th centuries, individual practitioners of astrology such as William Lilly (1602-1681) and John Gadbury (1627-1704) flourished in England. Lilly was exceptionally well-known in his day. He wrote *Christian Astrology*, the classic work on horary astrology, and was famous for predicting the Great Plague and the Fire of London.

Many astrologers of this period published almanacs or practiced horary astrology extensively. Also, astrological consultations for people other than the nobility became popular at this time. Attacks on astrologers increased, however, and came now from literary figures including Jonathan Swift. During this period astrology acquired a bad reputation, but the almanac with its star lore and astro-meteorological forecasts perpetuated some parts of astrology and became a regular part of daily life; its usage has survived to the present day.

A small revival of astrology occurred in the 1780s followed by another in the mid-19th century. The latter revival included a full range of astrological offerings, from popular astrological writings that were little more than "gossip columns" to serious texts. Only a few dedicated individuals in England and America kept the astrological lights burning during this dark period in astrology's long history.

Appendix III

The Twentieth Century

The rise of Theosophy in England during the later part of the 19th century stimulated a major revival of astrology that was led by Sepharial (Walter Gorn Old, 1864-1929), Alan Leo (1860-1917) and others. Many consider this to have been a mixed blessing because Theosophy, with its religious overtones, was completely rejected in scientific circles. But the astrological revival was sustained on a popular level, and during the first part of the 20th century astrological groups were formed in England, Germany, and the United States.

Alfred Witte (1878-1941) founded the Hamburg School of astrology (known in the U.S. as Uranian Astrology) and produced his book *Rules for Planetary Pictures* in the 1920s. Reinhold Ebertin (1901-1988) later developed Cosmobiology, a psychologically-oriented type of astrology which utilized some of Witte's ideas and took several new directions of its own.

In 1930, newspaper astrology was born in the London Sunday Express. In Ireland, Cyril Fagan (1896-1970), a founder of the Siderealist movement in astrology, researched the ancient origins of astrology and promoted the idea and location of the sidereal zodiac. In the 1950s, Michel (1928-1991) and Francoise (1929-2007) Gauquelin launched the most sophisticated statistical study of astrology ever attempted, demonstrating a link between planetary position and human nature. Around the same time John Addey (1920-1982) pioneered and developed the harmonic theory of astrology.

The United States soon became a center for the revival of most schools of astrology. Evangeline Adams (1868-1932) was the first superstar astrologer and captivated America with her radio show. C.C. Zain (Elbert Benjamin (1882-1951) published a series of influential books linking astrology with other occult sciences. Grant Lewi (1902-1951) popularized serious astrology by publishing periodicals and books. Strongly influenced by modern psychology, including the ideas of Carl Jung, the multi-talented astrologer Dane Rudhyar (1895-1985) developed what he called "humanistic astrology." Charles Jayne (1911-1985) brought a rigorous, analytical logic to the many technical problems of astrology. His cycle studies continue to be a major influence. The search for a physical mechanism that explains astrological influence was aided by the work of John Nelson, an engineer who worked for RCA for many years. He developed a method to forecast geomagnetic storms that was based on heliocentric positions of planets.

Concurrent with the rise of contemporary feminism in the 1970s, Eleanor Bach produced the first ephemeris of four asteroids named for Greco-Roman goddesses and established their symbolism. Also at this time Lois Rodden (1928-2003) began to establish a rigorous rating system for horoscopic data that has set the standard in astrological research. In the 1990s, Project Hindsight and ARHAT, independent translation projects, began to translate numerous ancient astrological texts that had never before appeared in English and have consequently stimulated an interest in ancient astrology. These are only some of the major contributors to astrology in the 20th century.

Mesopotamian and Non-Western Astrology

In the inhabited world of ancient times, four general regions saw the rise of great agricultural civilizations: Mesopotamia, India, China, and Mesoamerica. These four cultures produced great art, complex codes of conduct, religions, and philosophies to explain the meaning of life, as well as countless labor-saving devices that contributed to human progress. As would be expected, these civilizations had early on developed a sophisticated science based on close observation of the skies. This early science was a combination of astrology, astronomy, and calendrics. Successful agriculture, which requires the prediction of seasons, weather, and the counting of days, is made possible with this knowledge.

In Mesopotamia, history records the growth of cities and federations of cities along the Tigris and Euphrates Rivers as early as the fourth millennium BCE. In the valley of the Indus River at places like Harappa and Mohenjodaro, Indian civilization began in the third millennium BCE. The valley of the Huang Ho (Yellow River) was the place where Chinese civilization took form during the second millennium BCE, and along the Gulf of Mexico, near present-day Veracruz, Mesoamerica produced its earliest cities and cultural centers during the first millennium BCE. Each of these four regions tackled the challenge of measuring time in its own distinctive way and the astrological traditions that grew out of these earliest of scientific efforts are likewise unique.

Mesopotamia

As Westerners, we are most familiar with the astrological tradition of the West that is built on foundations laid in Mesopotamia thousands of years ago. In ancient times, skywatchers on ziggurats carefully observed the risings and settings of the sun, moon and planets and noted any phenomena occurring in human events that correlated with sky changes. They named the patterns of stars (the constellations) that the sun, moon and planets moved through and interpreted these constellations in terms of the cycle of life. Although there has been some considerable displacement between the seasons and the constellations over the past 4,000 or so years, the sequence of zodiac signs associated with the constellations correlates symbolically with the unfolding of the seasons of the year.

Our seven day planetary week and the planetary hours of astrology come from ancient Mesopotamia. In their system of counting time, and through natural observation, the day logically served as a primary unit. Counting 365 days for the year is unwieldy, so smaller units were created. Seven days is 1/4 the roughly 28-day cycle of the moon, and there were seven visible planets in ancient times (including the sun and moon); each of the seven days was named for a planet and said to be ruled by it

These planetary names are found today in the romance languages; English uses the Nordic equivalents of the Roman gods associated with each planet. Each day was further divided into 24 hours, 12 for daylight and 12 for night. These were unequal hours; they varied according to the length of the day as it changes during the year. But the system was essentially astrological because the hours were ruled by the seven planets in a definite order, the order of their average rate of motion against the sky (Saturn, Jupiter, Mars, Sun, Venus, Mercury, Moon). The seven planets that rule the hours repeat their order three times during the entire day and after 21 hours a new cycle begins, starting with another planet in the sequence. Whichever planet rules the first hour of the day, the hour after sunrise, gave its name to that day—hence, the names of the days and the sequential order of planets for the week are set. The system of planetary hours puts forth an astrology that names, and consequently gives meaning, to blocks of time. This same concept of planetary influence on time periods appeared in ancient China and Mesoamerica and formed the core of their astrological systems.

The astrology of Mesopotamia was also concerned with sky omens, especially those associated with the planets. Conjunctions and oppositions were observed in the clear, unobstructed skies of the ancient Middle East. They studied planets just rising or setting on the horizon; this emphasis survives as the Ascendant and Descendant points in the modern Western astrological chart.

When the Greeks rose to power in the region, they began to geometricize Mesopotamian astrology until it became almost entirely spatial. They added aspects, house divisions, and made the ecliptic-based 12-sign zodiac the showpiece of the system. Although much of what they did was built on older ideas, to them must go the credit for constructing a more rigorous system. By Roman times, astrology was a specialized discipline with a clear-cut methodology, described in books and practiced by experts. Today, this tradition is still very much alive and constantly evolving.

India

In ancient India, skywatchers learned to make calendars and predict where planets would be in the future. The *Vedas*, the sacred writings of ancient India, reveal a sky-knowledge that dates back to very early times. In 323 BC Alexander the Great extended his empire into parts of India and opened the floodgates for an exchange of cultures. Greco-Mesopotamian astrology found its way into India and influenced the form that Indian astrology eventually took. By the 3rd and 4th centuries AD the first Indian astrological treatises appeared, namely, *Yavanajataka* ("Greek Natal Astrology") by Sphujidhvaja, and

Vrddhayavanajataka ("Old Greek Natal Astrology") by Minaraja. By the time the great 6th century Indian astrologer Varahamihira published his masterwork on astrology, *Brihat Jataka* ("Great Natal Astrology"), the distinctive elements of Indian astrology were in place: a blend of ancient Vedic and GrecoMesopotamian astrology.

Today, Vedic astrology seems to be the preferred term for the indigenous astrology of India, the term obviously referring to the *Vedas*. In the recent past it has also been known as Indian or Hindu astrology. The Sanskrit name for the study of astrology (which in ancient times included mathematics and astronomy) is Jyotishastra ("science of the stars or light"). In India, Jyotish ("stars" or "light"), as it is commonly called, is taught in universities and practiced by professionals.

The exchange with Western astrology brought in the 12-sign zodiac, but in India its first point became attached to the constellation Aries, not the vernal equinox as has become the tradition in the West. Indian astrologers practice a sidereal astrology, placing the planets in signs that use the same names as in Western astrology, but are displaced from that zodiac by about 24 degrees. The distance between the two is called the Ayanamsha, a distance that is set officially by the government astrologer in India, although there is still debate among experts who use different figures.

The signs in Vedic astrology are called Rashis. The horoscope used in India, called the Rashi Chakra, is very similar to the square charts used by astrologers in Roman and Medieval times. Like Western astrology, Indian astrology became quite spatial and aspects and house positions are fundamental to the system.

Although Vedic astrology uses sign-based (which can have large orbs), rather than degree-based aspects, other techniques are employed that reveal subtle details about the distribution of the planets in the zodiac. Each zodiac sign is divided into thirds, fifths, sixths, sevenths, eighths, ninths, etc., similar to harmonics, which is derived from these "sub-charts" in Indian astrology. A chart called the navamsha chart, based on a division of signs into ninths, is commonly used in modern Vedic astrology to analyze marriage and relationships. It is also said to reveal one's deeper spiritual tendencies in addition to marriage karma. Essentially, this chart is a 9th harmonic chart and it treats novile aspects (a minor aspect of 40 degrees that most Western astrologers ignore) as conjunctions.

In India, one's Ascendant, called the Lagna, is considered the strongest point of personal identity. The Moon's nodes also play an important role in Vedic astrology: Rahu is the name for the north node, Ketu is the name for the south node. The Sanskrit names for the planets are as follows: Sun = Ravi; Moon = Chandra; Mercury = Budha; Venus = Sukra: Mars = Kuja; Jupiter = Guru; Saturn = Sani.

One unique and probably indigenous element in Indian astrology is found in the Nakshatras, the 27 lunar mansions, which are comprised of groups of fixed stars that lie close to the ecliptic. These are each 13°20' in length and begin at the first point of Aries. (Western, Chinese and Arabian astrological traditions contain what are often called lunar mansions or a lunar zodiac. In these systems the ecliptic is generally divided into 28 sections, each measuring 12°51'. Vedic astrology also has a system of 28 lunar mansions that are normally reserved for use in horary and electional astrology.)

The Nakshatra in which the Moon at birth is found is the foundation for perhaps the most interesting technique in Indian astrology, the computation of the Dashas, or planetary periods. In this forecasting technique, the spatial position of the Moon determines a sequence of time periods that affect the native throughout the course of life. In other words, space is turned into time. The Dashas are time-periods, blocks of symbolic time.

China

India was certainly influenced by Greco-Mesopotamian culture, but China, far more isolated, was much less so. In China, astrology took on forms very different from those in the West. The planets plus the Sun and Moon were not measured against the ecliptic-based zodiac; they were measured against the equator. The pole star was a point of great importance to the Chinese and it is the celestial equator, not the ecliptic, that relates to this point. Twenty-eight unequal lunar mansions on the equator, called Hsiu, divided the sky. The position of the Moon in each of these zones acquired a meaning. But this is about as far as Chinese positional or spatial astrology went. The real core of the system lies in an interplay of time cycles that may have originally been based on a combination of numerology and astronomical motions.

In very ancient times the Ten Celestial Stems, a sequence of ten consecutive symbols, became established as a symbolic cycle. Its most ancient origins may lie in the counting of fingers on two hands, or it may possibly also be a surviving artifact of an ancient ten-day week. Later the Twelve Terrestrial Branches, another symbolic cycle of stages—perhaps influenced by both the 12-year cycle of Jupiter and the division of the solar year into 12ths—was combined with the ten Stems to create a cycle of 60 days or 60 years. In a 60-day or 60-year period there are six cycles of the Stems and five cycles of the Branches. Each day or year in the cycle would then have two names, one for the Stem, one for the Branch. This sexagenary cycle applied to years is said to have been created by the legendary emperor Huang Ti in the year 2677 BC.

This same interplay of ten and twelve, using the same names, was also applied to months and hours. In the case of months, one year will, with adjustments, contain 12 months and therefore five years will yield 60 months. In terms of hours, five days of 12 hours each gives us the number 60 again. The year, month, day and hour of one's birth, the Four Pillars of Destiny as they are called, are then designated by a pair of names. Associations with the five elements of Chinese astrology (fire, earth, metal, water, and wood) and the polarities (yin and yang) further individualize the information about the birth moment. Today, Chinese astrologers still utilize this ancient system and almanacs are regularly published containing tables for determining the astrological qualities of any given day.

A full Chinese astrological reading takes into consideration more than just the Four Pillars of Destiny. The 28 lunar mansions or constellations are said to rule a day each, such that every four weeks of seven days begins the cycle anew. These constellations are said to indicate the element of chance and are used not only in interpreting a birth, but also for choosing auspicious days.

Another factor considered in a reading is the animal that rules the year of birth. This is a cycle of twelve years (not to be confused with the Twelve Terrestrial Branches), each year named for an animal and beginning with the Chinese New Year in early February. It is thought that this 12-year cycle is based on the cycle of Jupiter. The influence of the year of birth is said to denote the moral character of the person. This aspect of Chinese astrology has become quite popular in the Western world, but as we have seen, it is in reality only a small portion of a complex system.

Mesoamerica

We now come to the fourth, and least known, of the world's great astrological traditions, the time-based astrology of Mesoamerica. Around the time of the ancient Greeks (800 to 200 BC) a civilization known today as the Olmec flourished along the eastern coast of today's Mexico. Forerunners of the Maya, Toltecs, and Aztecs, the Olmecs built pyramids and ceremonial centers and also created a complex astro-calendrical system, portions of which have survived to the present day. During the Classic period of the Maya, when Europe was in its Dark Ages, this system evolved into one of the world's most sophisticated intellectual constructions. Scholars have long marveled at the precision achieved by the Maya in measuring the year and the cycles of the Moon. The purpose of all this astronomy was, however, to improve their astrology.

The Maya, Toltecs, Aztecs and other pre-Columbian cultures of Mesoamerica based their astrological analyses on the interplay of day-counts, not unlike the Chinese. They used a cycle of 13 numbers and a cycle of 20 signs which interfaced every 260 days (a figure equal to many astronomical cycles) as the core of their system. Also like the Chinese, they projected this cycle onto a larger frame of reference, dividing their creation cycle of 5,125 years (also called the Long Count) into 260 units of 7,200 days called katuns. The present creation cycle originated in 3114 BC and ended on December 21, 2012. Note that the Mayan creation cycle of 5,125 years is very close to 1/5th of the average cycle of Earth's precession, the movement that accounts for the shifting of the astrological ages described in Western astrology.

The key concept in Mesoamerican astrology is the notion of time as a sign. As we have already seen, the astrology of the West is mostly spatial. The most important yardstick in that system is determined by the signs of the zodiac, each sign measuring 30 degrees of space along the ecliptic. The astrological houses and the aspects are also spatial. A conjunction of planets or an eclipse is interpreted according to the sign in which it occurs. In ancient Mexico, however, astrologers interpreted a conjunction or an eclipse according to the 13-day sign in which it occurred, as well as other symbolic time frames.

Perhaps the most carefully watched planet in ancient Mesoamerica was Venus. Its 584-day synodic cycle was divided into four periods: inferior conjunction, morning star, superior conjunction, and evening star. The two appearance intervals of Venus—morning star and evening star—each last for 263 days on average. It has been suggested that this is one of several astronomical facts behind the selection of 260 as a master number in Mesoamerican astrology.

Mesoamericans believed that when Venus was conjunct the Sun and moving retrograde (the inferior conjunction), leaders would be struck down and there would be trouble in the land. They recorded the motions of Venus in books in the form of complex and very accurate tables. The Maya were well aware that five synodic cycles of Venus are equal to eight solar years and this knowledge formed an important part of their astrological-cosmological symbolism.

In terms of birth horoscopes, Mesoamerican astrology was similar to Chinese astrology. There was no circular chart as such, just a list of factors that needed to be considered in the analysis of character and destiny. First came the year of birth, one of four signs that were part of a 52-year cycle. Next were the 20 day-signs and the 13-day periods into which the birth fell. The day-sign, perhaps the most important and personal of the significators, was studied closely; it was often used as a part of a person's name. Each of these 20 signs was linked to one of the four directions, which function in many ways like the four elements in Western astrology. The ruler of the hour of birth and the phases of the Moon and Venus extended the interpretation. For mundane events, such as dedications and coronations, the stations of Mars, Jupiter, and Saturn were considered important factors in the quality of any given day.

Because the Spanish friars did a thorough job of eliminating anything they saw as pagan, we are not sure which factors were included in a traditional Mesoamerican astrological reading. What we do know of this great tradition is based mostly on the works of archaeo-astronomers and anthropologists. However, in remote parts of Mexico and Guatamala, an oral tradition has survived that retains some of the ancient astrological knowledge and is becoming better organized and more resistant to the constant pressures from Christianity. Academic researchers, practicing what they call ethno-astronomy, are also recording and documenting pieces of this lost knowledge.

Program for Applying Schools Equivalency Criteria

An applying school's curriculum would need to meet the criteria of NCGR-PAA's Study Guide. An applying school may meet only Level I, or Levels I and II, or they may meet Levels I, II and III. In the case of the last, an applicant would only need to apply for Level IV, and subsequently, professional certification. There would be no equivalency program for any school that would encompass Level IV certification, no matter if the school's curriculum included the material required for Level IV certification. Level IV must be taken to its completion by each applicant in their desired track of certification.

A school applying for Equivalency must submit a school purpose, description of the curriculum and the syllabus for each course taught. The grading system must be explained and how the classes are conducted.

The curriculum of an applying school must follow NCGRPAA's Study Guide guidelines and include the following:

Level I

The curriculum must provide building blocks of the foundation of Western astrology. The curriculum must provide a comprehensive education in the signs, planets, houses, personal points (Ascendant, Midheaven and Moon's Nodes); hemisphere emphasis and quadrants; major aspects and major configurations; and finally, the delineation of the topics listed.

An introduction in basic astronomical phenomena is necessary, such as retrogradation, eclipses and solstices. As well, the curriculum must be structured to provide proficiency in natal chart and planetary calculations for the northern and southern hemi-spheres, and east and west of Greenwich. It must introduce elementary material from Classical Astrology.

Level II

As well as the continuation and comprehensiveness of the criteria for Level I, the following must be added to the delineations:

    a. minor aspects

    b. lunar phases

    c. derived houses

    d. fixed stars

Calculations include:

    a. progressions (and their interpretation)

    b. solar arc directions (and their interpretation)

    c. the application of transits (and their interpretation)

    d. Vertex (and its interpretation)

    e. the Equatorial Ascendant (and its interpretation)

    f. antiscia (solstice points) (and their interpretation)

Mundane charting, such as ingress charts is required. Ancient and medieval astrology must have stronger coverage, as well as some other astrological disciplines, such as Vedic (Hindu) astrology.

Level III

For a school to meet the equivalency for Level III, the curriculum must thoroughly cover all the information included in Levels I and II. The curriculum must cover:

    a. the precise use the 360° and 90° dials

    b. horary and electional astrology

    c. synastry

d. solar and lunar returns

e. history

f. a survey of Vedic, Mesoamerican, and Chinese astrology

g. Classical astrology

An applying school for any Level of certification must meet the following criteria:

The school's instructor(s) must have a direct relationship with the student. This may be in a physical classroom; a private online site; via e-mail or telephone; or written correspondence.

There must be written homework, which includes essays, delineations, and calculations.

There must be exams that reflect the student's ability to recall subject matter.

There must be grades that reflect the student's attendance or participation, homework, and exams.

A graduate from an applying school may apply to NCGR-PAA's Education Director for approval, at which time the applicant may take the next exam he or she is authorized to take. The school must provide the applicant's transcript at the time of application.

NCGR-PAA Policy Re: Qualifying Schools for Equivalency

1. School needs to be officially in existence for at least five years.

2. School should have at least one graduating class.

3. School should be a stand-alone school; that is, not only strictly conforming to the NCGR-PAA curriculum, but have its own separate identity and curriculum.

4. School should have a faculty of at least three teachers.

5. School should have a program that spans at least two years. A series of workshops, seminars, lectures, etc. does not make a school. There should be some kind of comprehensive program of a continuous nature.

6. There should be a review, if deemed warranted, of an equivalency-granted school by the NCGR-PAA Education Director plus a chosen representative from the NCGR-PAA Board or the Board of Examiners after a five-year period from acceptance for equivalency. A school's equivalency will remain in force for as long as there is good will and cooperation shown between NCGR-PAA and the school.

7. The granting of equivalency for a school should be decided by the NCGR-PAA Education Director in consultation with the President and then voted final approval by the NCGR-PAA Board.

8. Some outside criteria should be established for equivalency, such as: APAI acceptance; state licensing; longevity and continuity of a school over a reasonable period of time; and other such considerations.

These requirements are over and above the criteria we now have in place as guidelines for equivalency, which are essentially a review of a school's curriculum of studies and a determination by the NCGR-PAA Education Director in consultation with the NCGR-PAA President as to the rigor of these studies. This entails a complete review of course topics covered within a school program, plus proof that applicants have successfully tested on those topics (transcripts or other such documentation). There should be some general conformity with NCGR-PAA's curriculum, as outlined in the NCGR-PAA Study Guide, in order to determine which NCGR-PAA Level can be exempted.

An applying school would not automatically be exempted from our Levels I, II, and III, but may be exempted from any one of these from Level I up. However, no school can be exempt from NCGR-PAA's Level IV exams.

The Formation of the NCGR Professional Astrologers' Alliance
NCGR-PAA

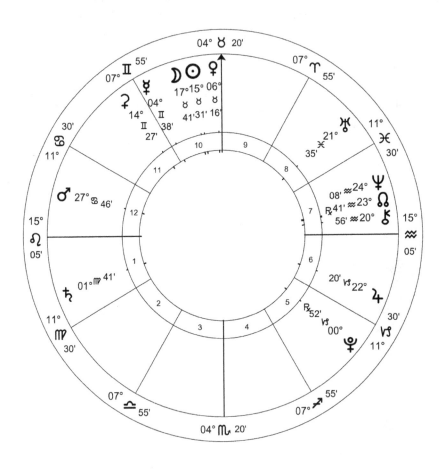

NCGR-PAA Foundation Chart May 5, 2008
11:57 AM EDT +4:00
Boston, MA, USA
42°N21'30" x 71°W03'37"

The Formation of the NCGR Professional Astrologers' Alliance

NCGR-PAA is a trade organization whose mission is to promote the common interests of astrologers and to improve the status of the profession of astrology primarily through the implementation of its certification program and publishing this accompanying curriculum and study guide; the promotion of ethical standards for astrologers; the offering of a professional empowerment program to provide the means for astrologers to improve their work and business practice through training and mentorship; and by way of any other matters relevant to the professional astrologer.

Incorporated in Boston on May 5, 2008 at 11:57 AM (see founding chart opposite), NCGR-PAA was formed as a result of a 2006 Internal Revenue Service audit, which determined that NCGR had strayed beyond its original stated goals by offering certification to astrologers and also through other services and programs that went beyond its educational and research purposes. Thus, NCGR-PAA is essentially an outgrowth of NCGR, and the two organizations share a common interest in serving the astrological community, each in its respective way. For example, while NCGR will continue its historic role as an educational and research organization, NCGR-PAA's certification program has been transferred in its entirety from NCGR, and all those astrologers who have been certified by NCGR are now NCGR-PAA certified. Those who have tested at various other Levels with NCGR now have their records transferred to NCGR-PAA.

As of this writing (2015), NCGR-PAA is still a work-in-progress, but the key word here is progress. Future plans include initiating a networking forum for members to discuss matters that impact their business operations. Opportunities to provide this forum will include the publication of e-zines, newsletters, and other periodicals, plus other forms of communication among astrologers, such as conferences or special events. NCGR-PAA will also initiate programs that reach out to the serious-minded astrological student or professional.

NCGR-PAA Study Guide

Notes

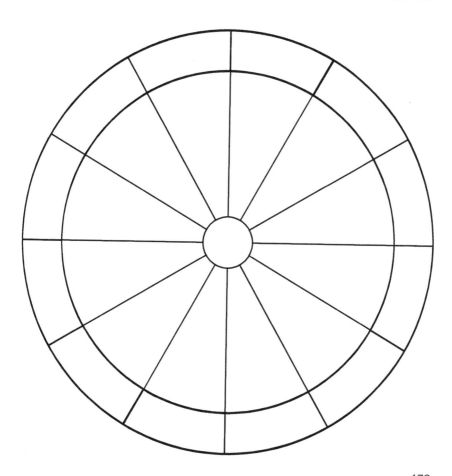

Printed in the USA
CPSIA information can be obtained
at www.ICGtesting.com
JSHW011637300923
49235JS00006B/25

9 780615 296395